THERE *are* KERMODIANS

THERE *are* KERMODIANS

A *liber amicorum* EDITED BY

ANTHONY HOLDEN &

URSULA OWEN

EVERYMAN

Published by David Campbell Publishers Ltd.,
Gloucester Mansions, 140a Shaftesbury Avenue,
London WC2H 8HD

Text © the authors, 1999
Design by Peter Campbell

ISBN 1-85715-997-7

Distributed by Random House (UK) Ltd.,
20 Vauxhall Bridge Road, London SW1V 2SA

Printed and bound in Germany
by Graphischer Grossbetrieb Pössneck GmbH

CONTENTS

ISLANDER

SHAPING SPIRIT

I

WORDS AND MUSIC

_____

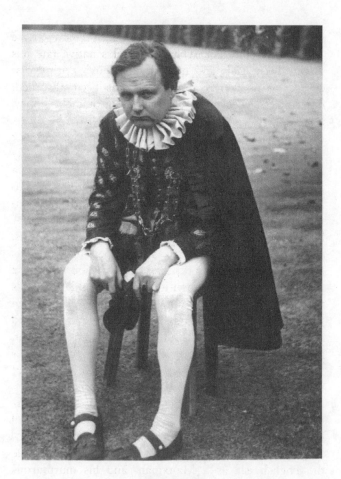

As Malvolio

1 . QUIET SUBVERSIVE

TO AN AMERICAN author, English reviews arrive after the fact, when the book's native fate has been dealt and more than enough critical discourse on its merits and defects has been absorbed; nevertheless, even tardy bees can sting or make honey. For years I was aware of Frank Kermode as the best English book reviewer – one who never fell into the cosy vice of cattiness or the casual shrillness that comes so easily to clever people reading and writing for low pay to a pressing deadline, one who seemed even at brief length to give fair if witty measure, one who seemed purposed neither to inflate the author nor to cut him down to size. A bibliophiliac geniality tempered his reviewer's doubts, and the professorial duty to grade papers tempered his enthusiasm. In the vanity fair of literary journalism he played the just, calm, omniscient man. And so it was that, during one of Kermode's fits of teaching in Cambridge, Massachusetts, I grilled a friend who had had him to dinner about the attributes of this exemplar, and was astonished to be told that he appeared to her 'perfectly nice', 'rather quiet', and even (the sense if not the phrase was here) 'cheerfully ordinary'.

Years later, in London in the late Sixties, I was personally to experience this paradox, of great erudition and cerebral flair carried modestly, even meekly. In his autobiographical writings he dwells upon his origins outside the English isle as a Manxman, and his murmurous social diffidence, his gentle lightness of manner, and the ruthless vengeance of his being a better critic than most anyone else all derive, one guesses, in some way, from that small outlying home, that fragment of old Viking empire east of Northern Ireland. He is, for all his decorum, an invader, a rogue, marking his career with a

9

certain restlessness and moments of rebellion. With admirable extracurricular energy he has persisted in keeping one voice active in the popular press and another actively enunciating scholarly discriminations of a fine, multilingual abstruseness, arriving at conclusions so calmly and colloquially couched that they seem inarguable – indeed just what we would have argued, had we troubled to know all that, or goaded ourselves to read this closely.

His sympathetic temperament, with its subversive undertow, unfurls itself most luxuriously in his love of the poets of the English Renaissance and in his concern, not quite loving, with the wrinkled, worm-holed texture of the Bible, a text whose historical claims upon close human study are quite obsolete for him, though for over two thousand years they generated a wealth of glosses that suit his intricate investigative purposes. He has the ability, anachronistic in an age of haughty, dismissive criticism that lords it over authors as the unwitting tools of past oppressions and misconceptions, to confess puzzlement, and to make his puzzling fruitful for the reader. I think, offhand, of his dwelling, in his consideration of *King Lear* as a classic, upon the brief exchange between Edgar and Gloucester whose most famous phrase, 'Ripeness is all', takes a flicker of possible intonations from its Shakespearianly crammed context – 'Perhaps the lesson,' Kermode speculates, 'isn't that "ripeness is all", but only that as long as you can still say that (or anything else), you have to hurry along, get on with life' – and of his pondering, in one of his guarded but charming pieces of self-description, why George Herbert hit upon a certain word, this inscrutable but successful choice containing the secret of poetry. The concepts of secrecy and error occur in his titles and recur in his works; the something finally unfathomable and indeterminate in Shakespeare constitutes, in Kermode's wonderfully attentive readings, the mark of the playwright's inexhaustible (from the standpoint of critics) genius.

Perhaps it is this recurrent humility, amid much certain knowledge and many incisive readings, which makes Kermode's criticism, unlike most, stimulating for a would-be creative artist. Just now, leafing through his writings on Shakespeare, I suddenly saw a way through a small crux in a work of mine in progress – the idea of a bold freedom in pursuit of a high dramatic excellence infected me. His criticism lent courage.

Kermode in his autobiography *Not Entitled* describes his inability to write a novel (a deficiency of presumptuous simple-mindedness, I would say, rather than of any other qualities) but the openness, the questingness, the several-sidedness of his criticism imply the courage and joy of creativity. His analyses enlarge rather than diminish, and heal rather than dissect. One of the first critics in the English-speaking world to grasp the import and worth of structuralism and its successor French modes of thought, he found himself compelled, in his long prologue to *An Appetite for Poetry*, to defend the continuing humanistic value of the classics and literary study against the radical devaluations of deconstruction and the absurd curricula that politically hip faculties offer the student body instead. Even in defence of what is most precious to him, however, so surprisingly and drastically undermined in recent decades by those presumably enlisted to preserve and expound it, Kermode's tone is level, respectful of the need for theory and renovation, and only incidentally wry.

But I meant merely to express birthday affection, not attempt an appraisal of an extensive and continuing career. Sharing on a few extended occasions proximate localities, and second wives who had much to say to each other, Kermode (accented on the first syllable, I learned) and I found ourselves with opportunities to make mutual observations, if not confessions. Men with access to other means of self-expression tend to hold their tongues.

Most of what I know about him I learned from reading his written words. What these words cannot quite convey is his mannerly lightness, and the sense he conveys of generous reserve – all the information and acuity, all the languages and internalised passages giving his foreground presence a resonating background. He has been knighted for his services to literature – a quaint fact for an American, implying crusades and legions of infidels. As one who perpetually feels guilty at not serving in our century's central crusade, which ended when I was thirteen, I am always aware of Frank's five years of wartime naval service, sailing under mad captains seas shared with 'people ruthlessly dedicated to the idea of ripping you apart or drowning you'. Yet he is funny. A sudden slant smile seems to announce the realisation that he is standing on a tipping deck. The years have translated the uncertainties of his provincial childhood and imperilled youth into a graceful diffidence proof against the shocks and deficiencies of old age.

As long as he can write for print, a high standard is being upheld in at least his instance. A decent devotion to literary merit and a humble and tenacious will to understand and explicate the best examples of it would not seem to be unattainable virtues. But this babbling, dumbed-down age makes them harder to attain than formerly, and their exponents rarer, with a touch now of the embattled heroic. Frank Kermode, since I first admired his book reviews nearly forty years ago, has been for me a hero.

John Updike

2. A SETTING OF ROBERT FROST'S
'THE SILKEN TENT'

guys it gently sways at ease.

and its supporting cen- tral ce-dar pole ____ that is its

pinnacle to heavenward and signifies the sureness of the soul, ____ seems to be

nought to any single cord, but strictly held by none, ____

14

loosely bound by countless silken ties of love and thought to every-

thing on earth the compass round,

and only by one's going slightly taut in

the Ca. priciousness of summer air is of the lightest bondage made aware.

Alexander Goehr

15

For Frank Kermode, who has told the world that the way to understand itself is to welcome interpretation and re-interpretation, till the end of time.

CELIA MORRIS met Zoe Lee her first week on campus. Zoe was tall, aggressively shy, with striking shiny black skin and cheekbones set high and angry. She was not beautiful, only large and austere; not gifted as a student, only desperately persistent. Celia was afraid of her, for some reason, and played with the idea of screening her out of the class. In the end she didn't have the nerve.

Everything scared Celia, her husband's death sitting on her so recent and so heavy. Michael Morris's death was one of those losses which strike whole communities. It hit me hard and I came into his orbit late in his career and life. It hit all of us – the designers, the writers, directors, the painters, an actor – such as myself – who relied on Michael Morris for more than just professional financial advice. We received from him what I can only call grace: a humane address to the crazy, crushing world of theatre and writing and art. If we were so badly struck down how much more would Celia be wiped out. We watched and waited.

Celia couldn't afford to wait. In his caring so eloquently and elegantly for all of us, Michael had not taken care to become rich or even mildly plush. I think that since we all assumed he would always be there for us, he picked up on the loony idea of his own immortality. It was typical of him. The security of the people who made the beautiful things he admired so much was more important than his own. So his financial wit died with him. And Celia, the wife of the attorney-at-law to the arts, inherited the fate more common to the widows of artists and scientists: she was broke. Still dazed by what had happened to her she had to go back to teaching college English at the City University.

Now all this was in the rough-and-tough days of the Sixties in New York. Campuses were crowded, issues flamed on every walk and lawn; the placard and the bullhorn were as basic as books. Through the whirling chaos Celia walked, oblivious. Everyone's personal history must intersect with the general condition. And if one is more intense the other gives way. Before the grief of losing Michael Morris those dramatic campus events gave way. Celia was a ghost haunted by ghosts.

Still there was registration. Nothing is as real as registration. And nothing rouses the half-dead as well as a roiling group of students raising questions about a class you've only half thought through. With relief Celia realized she could still do it. She talked about the need for all kinds of literature, relevant (and irrelevant? she wondered) as well as more distantly applied fictions. She seized on two Jameses, James Baldwin and Henry James.

This done, she divided the class along voluntary lines – it was the fashion of the hour – and the blacks and Puerto Ricans clustered into one group, the lower middle class and a smattering of middle-class whites in the second. While they executed a writing assignment Celia felt herself begin to menstruate; she was near tears. That was all supposed to be over. But she'd been irregular ever since her thirties: a special case, the gynaecologist had said. It was a bad joke to be reminded that you were alive so soon after everything had died.

She cut the assignment short. Zoe Lee towered over her, a shadow cutting off her light. She was the first to hand in her paper. Thanks for nothing, Celia thought, staring down the sullen young woman. This is a first for me, Celia thought, hating a student. And one who's done nothing to me. Grief makes you crazy, she decided.

It made her drunk that night in a half-hour flat. Robe on, Tampax in – she sat on the carpet in the living room, shoes kicked off, dinner-less, glass in hand and tried to read papers. But the room was full of echoes, distractions. In the corner the piano sang silently, sang the Schubert G Major Sonata which Paul Badura-Skoda had played twenty years earlier. (The pianist had been grateful – saved by Michael's skill from what he'd called his financial death wish.) It became the family joke – all these gifted men and women saved from financial suicides by Michael Morris, a roly-poly British lawyer who loved the artist and the arts so deeply he could see no difference between them. And they loved him back, making his home an oasis of song, poetry and general conversation which even that confused time recognised as extraordinary.

Celia built a fire and crowded out music, laughter and the delicious debris of the past by reading papers. Zoe Lee's paper jumped out at her. It was awful! The term 'broken English' usually reserved for foreigners came to her mind. 'Writing means to have a thing in which you be told what things mean in the world ....'

God, she thought, this class is going to be murder. She rambled through the two Jameses and chose two stories: 'Sonny's Blues' by James Baldwin and 'Brooksmith' by Henry. She would not blaze trails. She would act out the cliché. The blacks get Baldwin the whites get James. No illusions with either group. 'Sonny's Blues' was an elegiac tale of a gifted black man and his troubled younger brother who, finally, he could not save. 'Brooksmith' was the tale of a butler at one of those Jamesian salons of the imagination, so spoiled by the quality of the discourse at his master's evenings that he cannot survive the man's death and all that vanishes with it.

Some sane, still sober part of Celia knew she was attracted by the echo of her life with Michael. Brook-smith, like dear, round, appreciative Michael, was an artist without an art, attending those who owned and exercised the gifts. These days any echo would do. She took it and fell asleep on the floor in a blur of books.

The next day she zombied through both sections of the class, assigning the stories and trying not to look at Zoe Lee who, in any case, turned out to be absent. After lunch she was almost knocked down in the hallway by Zoe Lee.

'What ... what is it?'

'I couldn't get to class.' Her famous icy aplomb was gone. 'What was the assignment?'

Celia told her and watched the tall ghost flee towards the exit.

C wonders what Z has on her that shakes her up so. They're as far apart in lives as in the alphabet – though Celia knows nothing of Zoe's life. She sleeps badly that night, and doses heavily with coffee the next day. She writes the assignment briskly on the blackboard:

SONNY'S BLUES BY JAMES BALDWIN

Write eight hundred words on theme, etcetera, etcetera ... A hand shoots up instantly. Celia's fears confirmed. It is, of course, Zoe.

'What is it, Miss Lee?'

'But you say "Brooksmith" by Henry James.'

'I said – what?'

'When I asked you in the hall ...' Celia is shaken. What a dumb mistake. I am going crazy, she thought. I have to get away. I started working too soon after death. Black is the colour of mourning. Z is the last letter of the alphabet. You need more time, she tells herself.

To Zoe Lee she said, 'All right', trying to sound professorially certain. 'Have you read "Brooksmith"?'

'Yes, I have.'

Amazement arrives that night. It is the vodkas and the heavyweight wine which overwhelm her lightweight tuna fish dinner and leave her lightheaded. It is not a phantasm. The only paper on any topic that was worth a damn was Zoe Lee on Brooksmith. Passionate, intelligent, infused with an offbeat but central understanding of the tale, even the awful locutions could not destroy it, could not wipe out Celia's sense of discovering something, someone.

'Brooksmith be spoiled by being only part way into the beautiful world of his master Mister Offard. It can be a curse on you, they let you in part way so you can't go back and they hate for you to go forward.'

'This is a very good paper.'

'Good,' Zoe Lee said. Ice! But Celia was hot on the trail.

'It's so much better than the first one. Why?'

'The first was just to talk smart so I could get into the class.'

'What's your direction, Zoe?'

'What?'

'What do you want to do?'

'A nurse. I have to be a nurse.'

'I see. But, still, it's so unusual to do such a good paper out of the blue. James is not an easy writer.'

'I don't care about your writers,' Zoe Lee said. 'I never heard his damn name before you.' Her eyes burned with the blind intensity that had been scaring the hell out of Celia. 'I am Brooksmith,' she said.

And it all poured out. She lived with her mother and three sisters in Bedford Stuyvesant. They were all prostitutes. Her sisters thought she was crazy for wanting a different life. Her mother was in a rage against her – hoping she would fail.

'I ain't going to do it and keep on doin' it for no man I don't know and just wants my ass – and get beat up like my sister Adelia so she have a hurt in her kidney all the time after. I am going to be a nurse.'

And she told Celia how she felt spoiled, like Brooksmith. She had no real place any more but she didn't want to be left beind like him, to die. Astonishing Celia again, she wept. When the white woman tried to touch her hand in confusion and consolation, Zoe Lee stood and towered over her.

'You'll be able to do it,' Celia said. 'Why shouldn't you?' She could hear the ring of nothingness in her voice. So could Zoe Lee.

'What the hell are you here,' she said. The contempt that rang in her voice may have been precisely what Celia had feared all along, who knows?

'It's not your damned class. I can't hardly do the science class. They the ones I need for the nursing. What the damned shit you know about it!'

'I didn't say I know …'

"Everything come easy to you …'

'That's not true.'

Celia is hurt and feels, at the same time, foolishly formal. She takes a breath and can hardly believe what she is confiding.

'I'm having a terrible time and you know nothing about it.'

'I know your man is dead. Whole class knows that …'

Celia is ready to give up.

'That's not your business.'

Control returns. 'I will try to help you. I want to help.'

'Yeah –' Zoe wipes her eyes with a tissue.

Celia can handle no more of this insane unwarranted intimacy. It's already more than she's counted on. She was up to a quick compromise, no more. She feels sweaty, exhausted.

'Then perhaps,' she says, 'we understand each other –

and we can go on from here.'

But going on is always more difficult than it seems. Celia was determined to do the right thing by this extraordinary young woman. We've been spoiled, she thought. We've both of us been spoiled. She'd arranged a science tutor for Zoe, had given her a good grade in the literature seminar and, at the last, lost track of her; as one does, finally, of just about all students, even those who raise questions about one's own life.

Four years after her first encounter with Zoe, Celia entered the hospital for an operation, nature uncertain. I had called her for reasons of my own; my acting life was drying up to a point I could no longer afford to ignore. I was playing with the idea of teaching drama at a university until a summer stock job came through, and I wanted Celia's advice.

When the department secretary told me of her illness I went to visit her. We had not been close for a long time. But I still thought about the old days – the perfect evenings – when Michael was alive. Since he'd died things had not been the same for me, either, not only socially but financially. In fact a lawyer and an accountant had helped get me into precisely the kind of mess Michael was so exquisitely adept at keeping me out of. So, as Freud says of dreams, my visit was over-determined.

I found Celia quite excited. 'Listen,' she said. 'There's a student of mine here.'

'Oh?' The room was empty.

'Across the hall.'

'Is it serious?'

'She's a nurse.'

And she told me, lying there in her flowered nightgown, the story of Zoe Lee; just the way I've told it here. Then she led me on a foray to find Zoe Lee. Zoe was, as advertised, tall, strikingly midnight-black and austere.

She was making some entries on a chart and looked up at us.

'Hello, Zoe,' Celia said.

She looked down at us, coolly. 'You know me, Ma'am?' The 'Ma'am' must have been an acquired piece of post-nursing school politesse. 'How do you know my name?'

'You were my student.'

'What class was that?'

'English. Your first year. Don't you remember? You wrote that wonderful paper.' Celia was shaky on my arm; I could feel her rigid, trembling. 'It was on a story by Henry James – "Brooksmith". And you told me –'

I wanted to stop Celia but there was no way.

'You said –', Celia raised her voice in proud imitation, 'I am Brooksmith!' The phrase hung in the air for a moment.

At last Zoe Lee allowed herself a small smile. It lit up nothing.

'I remember you. You're Mrs Morris.'

'Yes,' Celia said. 'I see you've done what you set out to do. You're a nurse.'

Zoe permitted herself a nod. 'But I never said anything about any Brooksmith. I don't know that name.'

'Brooksmith?'

'I remember your class. We read James Baldwin. "Sonny's Song", some title like that.'

'"Sonny's Blues."'

'That's right. Well, I have patients to tend.'

And she was gone. Celia was inconsolable. I saw, too, that she was sicker than I'd let myself notice. She was weak, one eye half-closed. In the next half-hour she reviewed everything: Zoe Lee, her lost Michael, their life together, then Zoe all over again, on some endless loop of memory.

'How could she have forgotten?'

'It was only a story assignment to her,' I said, stupidly.

'Oh, no,' Celia said. 'You don't understand.'

Celia was stuck in the hospital for a long course of treatment. But she made some phone calls for me and, during the next few weeks, with her help, I began to mend my frayed life by working as a substitute teacher of drama. Not being a true academic I found myself with a certain unconventional freedom. And, for some perverse reason, I read 'Brooksmith' – the little story which had caused such an upheaval in Celia's sense of things. And, still more perversely, I assigned it to my class. Write five hundred words on the central dramatic conflict ...

More importantly, I felt a kind of intimate acquaintance with the taciturn British servant. Being exiled myself from my theatrical past – a past which had shed its glamour long ago, but which I still missed – I could understand him. I suppose I felt spoiled in my own way. I'd had my moments. The *Times* reviewer once said I had a certain grace. And I'd played in Pinter at the Royal Shakespeare, a long time ago, and Pinter himself had said I was 'strong'. And here I was teaching drama to students whose idea of tragedy was the violent death of rock stars. To push myself on I plunged into it with a high seriousness, research and all. And made an interesting discovery.

I found the buried roots of Brooksmith.

EXCERPT FROM THE NOTEBOOKS OF HENRY JAMES

Another little thing was told me the other day about Mrs Duncan Stewart's lady's maid, Past, who was with her for years before her death and whom I often saw there. She had to find a new place of course, on Mrs S's death, to relapse into ordinary service. Her sorrow, the way she felt the change and the way she expressed it ...

'Ah, yes ma'am, you have lost your mother, and it's a great grief, but what is your loss to mine? You continue to live with clever, cultivated people: but I fall again into my own class. I shall never see such company – hear such talk – again. She was so good to me that I lived with her, as it were; and nothing will ever make up to me for the loss of her conversation. Common, vulgar people now; that's my lot for the future.'

I read this late one night, wonderfully struck by the possibilities of transformation. So Brooksmith had been something, someone, before becoming a perfect but spoiled butler in the perfect salon. He had been a lady's maid named Past with a sensibility above her station. Then why not a Brooklyn black trying to escape the prostitute's fate? And who could know what he'd be the next time?

I felt oddly excited. I was not too played out, too lost, to be beyond discovering something. I'd unearthed some sort of permanent patron saint of aristocratic nostalgia. The morning couldn't come soon enough. I was eager to share my find with Celia. But when I got to the hospital I found she'd taken a turn for danger in her illness. She could not register who was visiting her – and her fever was high. I hesitated at the door; an oxygen tent inhaled and exhaled. A black form shook a thermometer, cranked the bed. The next time I came, early the following evening, Zoe Lee was still hovering over Celia, as if she were caring for a mother. I asked the head nurse at the station about it, as indirectly as I could.

'Ah, Zoe and Mrs Morris,' she said. 'Zoe's pulling her through. Every day a little more, a little better.'

'Really …'

'Well, they were old friends, it seems,' the head nurse said. 'Zoe asked to be put on her case when she heard about Mrs Morris's condition. And Zoe is in great demand; everyone has an eye on that young woman. She's special, Zoe is. Self-educated, too. Extraordinary.'

'Yes,' I said. 'So I see.'

Daniel Stern

25

Gabriel & Raphael spin round Pauls
Heavenly Haydn crotchets the walls,
Chaos & Light roll away,
Echoes drowning from night to day.

Before the choir sits Frank Kermode
Waiting before Joseph in worshipping mode,
He breaks the cuts to Adam & Eve
Chucked, shoved, without reprieve.

Next in a stand at the mighty Gooners
Leicester holed by one of many bloomers
We stop in a lay by on the way home
Listening to a race, leaker whips moan.

Sometime later to 'Dadie' at Kings
A memorial service sans extra things
Paradise Purcell was certainly thee
His setting of Quarles, for whom it doesn't cue

Dr Frank you grow younger by the day.
If I knew your secret, I'd certainly pay
Is it monkey glands, or ancient carp's liver
That keep you a youth, while I stoop & shiver?

This my recollection for his liber amicorum
Notted memories of a man whose forum
Is that bristling fortress academe
Where I can't be heard & will never be seen

Robert Tear

5. AFTERWARDS

I HAVE KNOWN Frank the whole of my adult life. Longer really, because I was a brash Oxford undergraduate when I first met him and far from being an adult. This was around 1950, when I founded a student literary club called the Oxford University Critical Society. The purpose of the club was to promote the 'New Critics' – Richards, Empson, Blackmur, Brooks, etc – whose analytic approach to literature was strenuously resisted by most of the traditionalists who ran the Oxford English faculty. Frank and John Wain – then both teaching at Reading – were among the first people who came to talk to us.

Unlike Wain, who always wanted to be centre stage, Frank was – and still is – modest and self-deprecating, ironically gloomy, always expecting the worst and responding to praise with 'Who? Me?' surprise. But his baffled incompetence was all a show. He was astonishingly knowledgeable; he had read all the books and all the books about the books, as well as the learned articles; he knew the facts, the texts, the variations and emendations. This in itself was not altogether unusual in the academic world; universities are full of learned scholars, each of whom knows everything there is to know about some tiny unaired corner of knowledge. But Frank's scholarship was altogether different, and not just because he took it for granted and made it look easy. He also showed that it was possible to know everything about, say, a poem by Donne and still be shaken by the experience of reading it. More important, he seemed to have been impelled to find out about the poem because it had shaken him. He was equally passionate about classical music and unusually knowledgeable, yet whenever he was presented with a work he hadn't heard before, the first thing he did was read the programme notes, as

27

though he would listen better if he knew the historical context. Scholarship was a habit of mind for him, but it was always secondary to his love of art itself.

Frank served in the Navy during the war and the Navy had taken him to Iceland, America, Australia, Algeria – places he had probably never dreamed of visiting when he was growing up on the Isle of Man. So he understood that there was a world outside the universities, a world with different priorities, which he respected and admired. And I admired him for that, too, or maybe I envied him because travelling was difficult back then at the beginning of the Fifties, and all I knew of the world elsewhere was what I'd picked up during a five-week spell at Grenoble University.

When Frank and I first met the study of English was not academically respectable. English was like geography or forestry, a subject students read if they weren't up to tackling serious disciplines such as the classics or mathematics or the sciences. So far as Oxford was concerned, scholarship was the only way in which this down-market discipline could acquire a little academic prestige. It was this patronising attitude to a subject I loved which inspired the Critical Society. We wanted to show that the New Criticism was a serious intellectual alternative, if only because it required students to think about the texts in front of them and try to find out what made them work. Our favourite quotation was from Empson's *Seven Types of Ambiguity*: 'Critics, as "barking dogs" ... are of two sorts: those who merely relieve themselves against the flower of beauty, and those, less continent, who afterwards scratch it up.' The key word was 'afterwards': first you reacted, then you gave your reasons why that particular poem or novel had moved you. In the first flush of the discovery that it was possible to talk about a poem without using the word 'magic', criticism became for us a high-minded calling, strenuous, respectable and even more alluring than creative writing itself. The poet or novelist was just the poor schmuck who provided the texts; the critic explored their depths and explained what they really meant.

This style of fighting talk divided English departments into two warring camps: scholars who knew everything about texts and their authors but couldn't tell good from bad, and critics who made judgements and weren't bothered by boring details and facts. Frank was the great exception: a shrewd and discerning critic and also a superb scholar who went on to produce authoritative editions of major writers.

And that is how he has remained. Despite his incomparable learning and grand professorships, the knighthood, the roll-call of honorary degrees from famous universities, he has never acquired the king-of-the-castle arrogance that often goes with academic eminence. This may be because, as I've said, he is a modest, private, worldly man who has an interesting life outside academia – a life where learning doesn't count for so much. But there is a more fundamental reason: he is too involved in literature to put on airs. Because he is a fine critic and understands what he reads from the inside, he knows that feelings are always mixed and motives ambiguous, and he applies this knowledge to his own life. Although he himself may not have written novels or poems, he is full of authorly self-doubt. His intellectual world is peopled, like Eliot's, by 'men whom one cannot hope to emulate' and he judges his own achievements accordingly.

I also owe Frank a personal debt: he is the only man in England ever to have offered me a regular job – at Reading University. As it happens I went to America instead and since then Frank has been my only steady link with the academic world. Since then, too, talking to him about poetry – especially about the seventeenth century poetry we both love – makes me realise how much I have missed: the pleasure of swapping quotes, conversing in shorthand without having to explain the references, the pleasure of the mutual obsession.

But when Frank talks about academic power struggles and what has happened to teaching now that theory, politics, race and gender have replaced the study of literature for its own sake, my admiration for my old friend turns into wonder. I have always loved him for his subtlety and self-deprecation and effortless learning. But how he has managed to go his own stylish way and hang on to his belief in literature as a living art – as voices in the reader's head, images in the mind's eye, imaginary presences with lives of their own – that is altogether beyond me.

Al Alvarez

6. ONCE HEARING MUSIC

Once hearing music, I thought: A man or woman made
this. And once there was a time before its pattern was.
Before its form or harmonies had ever been conceived

Out of flesh and its travails. Out of the labour of hands.
And before that, a time when not one single quaver
of it had been the slenderest shadow. Less even than a
shadow

Lying dark in its maker. Until it was shaped, crafted and
nourished into light. And he or she no angel but human
to the core. Who made it for you, for me, that we

Might see clear through it, build our own work upon it,
and by our willing love, also transform our world. That
through us, matter be known, transparent and resplen-
dent

As music. And with these thoughts, I rejoiced to be in its
history, to be alive in its time: my time now his and hers.
And yours too, as you hear this. Which is not the time its
maker

Lay less than a pip in an apple, unformed, unborn,
unnamed. Yet to you and me in our times that maker of
music reached out. And me here humanly touched. And
moved to make this.

From *The Manager*

Richard Burns

7. A SENSE OF A BEGINNING

DOING WHAT I then thought of as research for my A-level text, *The Tempest*, I read a new book called *Renaissance Essays* by someone I then thought of as Frank Kermode. It seemed to me, not exactly used to books like that, to be at once astonishingly learned and engaged with its subject, and lucid in an ordinary way. As though one could learn something without intimidation being involved. And unlike the impassioned Leavisite teaching of literature that I had had – and loved, it should be said – it didn't need to think its subject was important in order to think that it was interesting.

Ten years later, having read what was then called Literature at university, and having finished a training in child psychotherapy, I thought of writing a book on Winnicott; and that I would call it *Inscrutable Whims*. I thought this title that I had come up with was rather stagey and pretentious – but good. I thought, in that exhilarating way in which one can sometimes justify oneself, that it linked Emerson – who had wanted to write WHIM above the door of his study – and Winnicott, who seemed from his writing to be more genuinely intrigued by other people than any psychoanalyst I had read; and that meant seeing and liking just how whimsical people are. Both Emerson and Winnicott seemed more interested in travelling than arriving, which made them subtler in their apprehension of erotic life, about which they seemed to be relatively unconcerned; and both were fascinated by how one thing – a mood, a feeling, a belief – turns into another, by the enigma of transitions. Anyway, *Inscrut-able Whims* was what it was going to be; the phrase seemed the key to something, and it had the added ad-vantage of sounding vaguely like Wallace Stevens, or Marianne Moore. Indeed, it did occur to me at the time that it might be, like most of one's best phrases, a quotation.

Around this time someone suggested to me that I should write to Frank Kermode to find out if I could write a Fontana Modern Master on Winnicott. I had read his books, as they had come out, so this seemed a daunting and entirely plausible idea. I had recently written a short piece on tickling, which I sent him along with a synopsis. Frank Kermode replied return of post; 'no one wants to tickle old men; your paper made me realise how much I miss it. Do come and talk to me.' Our meeting was remarkably easy, and enjoyable; and I thought that if nothing else writing the book would be a good enough pretext to go on meeting. But there was one false note. I mentioned, in passing, that I had wanted, originally, to write a book on Winnicott called *Inscrutable Whims*. I noticed – or thought that I had noticed; it was never referred to again – the faintest smile of embarrassment. I was left with an awkwardness, but I just assumed that I had so wanted to impress, that any bit of unease between us could have haunted me.

As I wrote the book it became clearer and clearer to me just how important the whole notion of transition was for Winnicott. Indeed his most radical theoretical contribution was the idea of the transitional object that makes possible the child's ongoing transitions between the mother and whatever else is not the mother. The object, the teddy bear, or piece of material, signifies development because it signifies two-way traffic. The child has to be able to come and go in order to be able to do either. And this, as Winnicott shows, is a life-long process. It was then curious to be rereading Frank's *The Sense of an Ending*, to find this:

But there is one important element in this apocalyptic pattern which I have as yet hardly mentioned. This is the myth, if we can call it that, of Transition. Before the End there is a period which does not properly belong either to the End or to the saeculum preceding it. It has its own characteristics.

When I say it was curious to come across this again – and *The Sense of an Ending* had been a kind of cult book for me, and still is – I mean that it was unsettling to discover circuits of influence in play, radars of affinity working away despite oneself. How much, in Winnicott's language, one 'uses' other people, depends upon them unwittingly, to discover one's own directions. It is always slightly uncanny when one gets a glimpse of what it is – or who it is – one has been relying on.

In writing this for Frank I decided to read again his early books that had been, one way and another, so important to me. Just what it is that sustains people's interest, what makes a so-called classic, has, after all, been one of Frank's abiding preoccupations. Whether it has been through the peculiar dream-work of scholarship, or the more evidently pragmatic work of journalism, it has been the often dark arts of transmission – what people pick up from each other to carry on with – that Frank has been so consistently eloquent about. In an essay called 'Shakespeare's Learning' I came across this:

Shakespeare's most obviously learned work ... belongs to the periods when he was young and *désoeuvré* and trying a different role from the one he settled in; or when he was indulging the inscrutable whims of his last phase in *The Tempest*. He was first a scholar to please patrons, and last a scholar to please himself; in between he was a scholar to please no one.

If the last sentence is a fine formulation of what, at its best, an education should be for everyone, the very title of the essay is a kind of emblematic drama. For 'inscrutable' the *Oxford English Dictionary* has 'That cannot be searched into or found out by searching; impenetrable, unfathomable; entirely mysterious'. For 'whim' it has 'a fanciful or fantastic creation ... A capricious notion or fancy; a fantastic or freakish idea'. The verb means 'to desire capriciously ... to be giddy'. Whatever else an inscrutable whim might be it speaks of the mysteries of inheritance, of not knowing where things come from, and of knowing they must come from somewhere. To indulge in such things is, one might say, to hint at new kinds of pleasure; pleasures, Frank intimates, that Shakespeare was experimenting with in his last play. And thereby adding yet another sense of an ending.

There is a kind of influence that is a benign version of stalking, in which one doesn't so much knowingly and intently follow someone, as discover that one has been following up on something. It is an unwitting form of collaboration – Freud called it dream-work – and it seems to be the way one's affinities work themselves out; one's affinity with oneself realised through unnoticed affinities with others. There is rather little anxiety in this version of influence, and more the pure pleasure of being given a good start, for something of one's own. That is what I seem to have got so often from Frank. For such things one feels fortunate.

Adam Phillips

2

HANGING ABOUT WITH FRANK

———————

In Italy with Deborah Kermode and Brian Phelan

8. STRICTLY BALLROOM

Only God, my dear,
Could love you for your mind alone
And not your dancing flair.

EVERYONE KNOWS about Frank's extraordinary talent as a scholar, thinker and critic. I too have benefited from his gift for close reading of texts – in this case, psychoanalytic ones. He knows an unreasonable amount about psychoanalysis, given that he's never tried it!

What I love most about talking with him, though, is not just the effortless intelligence and charm, but something else: he is a man of quite extraordinary grace – intellectual, physical and vocal. Indeed, he has one of the loveliest voices I know – light, expressive, and faintly resonant. His tone is always mild, except when he is disturbed by lapses he can't abide – by irrationality and insensitivity. Then his voice becomes a little thin, a little high, and you hear a note of disbelief and mildly irritable pleading. He is not enraged, just deeply bewildered by the lack of sweet reason and order in the world. I can't imagine him ever shouting about it. I sometimes wish he would.

Back in 1973, he and his second wife Anita, her son Davey, another family and ours went to Italy together for Christmas and New Year. On New Year's Eve the gang of us trooped up to a restaurant in a small village on the top of a Tuscan mountain, and we spent the whole evening dancing. More than the evening – we literally tangoed and polkaed the night away. Frank, of course, loves music, once played the violin, and has a fine ear for the movement of poetry and prose, but it is all there in his heels too. His leading is light and totally natural, and he has a sense of rhythm to die for. I remember wild gaiety in the polkaing. He is a dream of a dancer. I hope we manage a few turns more before we all say goodnight.

Anne Alvarez

9. VOYAGING

THEY'D DRESSED thoughtfully for arrival in Canberra, I saw, as they came down the steps from the aircraft. She walked gracefully on her high-heeled riding boots. Both were sporting large and shiny stetsons, and looked as if they might well be armed. Something in the man's walk, however, and the faintly parodic angle of his hat suggested a milder temperament. Beneath the stetson was a well-known English literary critic who'd just flown in from St Louis, Missouri, for a two-day seminar organised in his honour by the ANU's Humanities Research Centre. It was November 1988, and the Kermodes were to spend a couple of weeks in Canberra. I took Anita immediately to some nearby stables, as she was anxious to put her riding boots to practical use. Happily on horseback, she disappeared into the pine forest by the lake, where she was to pass many hours during the days that followed. Frank meanwhile took off his stetson and got down to work.

The HRC seminar was on the subject of 'History and Value'. It coincided with the Australian publication of Frank's book of that title, and of a novel by Stephen Haggard called *Nya*, first published in 1938 and now almost totally forgotten, that had been reissued by OUP at Frank's prompting with an introduction by him. In the two related sets of lectures (Clarendon and Northcliffe) which Frank had given in England the previous year and had now united under the title *History and Value* he'd pondered the seemingly mysterious way in which certain literary works, like certain episodes within an individual life, manage to endure – within a literary canon, within a human memory – while others, equally mysteriously, do not. What gives these works, these episodes, their value? How are our personal histories interwoven with the larger intellectual histories we try to construct? Why were questions of value so slightingly regarded by literary critics at the present time? These were matters we also wanted to explore at the Canberra seminar.

For his Clarendon lectures Frank had chosen to speak about 'bourgeois literature in the Thirties'. He'd wryly observed at the outset that the literature of the Thirties 'happened to be the modern literature of my own youth', and that as most of his present audience were aged about twenty they'd have the pleasure of witnessing a piece of living history, someone who'd actually been about at the time and could explain – might indeed need to explain – why a particular work had meant something to him then, though it was now more generally neglected. He'd begun the case with *Nya*, persuasively describing the strange charm and power the book had held for him – now though in a necessarily more muted way. He'd analysed with equal acuteness the possible reasons for the book's present neglect: the curious innocence, the docility, with which it handled its potentially transgressive theme of a love affair between a man in his middle twenties and a thirteen-year-old girl who'd returned to the constraints of England after a childhood of joyful freedom in Nyasaland. One reason he liked the book, he supposed, was because it treated its explosive subject with such utter calm; but such calmness (he realised now) was also perhaps indicative of its larger social evasiveness, of questions it refused to address.

There was perhaps some connection in Frank's thinking, though he never made it explicit, between that aspect of the novel which he'd chosen chiefly to discuss – the disparity in the ages of the lovers – and that other disparity that he'd lightly referred to in the preface to his lectures, between the age of the lecturer who'd lived through the Thirties and that of his younger audience who knew nothing at first hand of that decade, but had come – despite that, because of that – to listen and learn. In the novel this experiential gap is negotiated by love: by the curious junction of the young girl's passion and the calmer knowledge of the older man. In teaching and writing – well, here the relationship would be different, no doubt, but a negotiation of sorts would still (it seemed) be required, as 'history' was slowly constructed and 'value' progressively considered; and the element of affection, of romance, of mutual openness, seemed vital here as well.

But there were considerations of place as well as time – so I came to think, in the course of Frank's Australian visit – which might be significant in relation to the larger argument that he was pursuing in these lectures, and indeed to the particular case of *Nya*. 'Geography' was the unspoken third term that needed perhaps to be thought of alongside 'history' and 'value'. In *Nya* romance is generated as much by the difference in the two lovers' backgrounds (of Nyasaland and England) as by their difference in ages. That novel is much concerned with voyaging, and much of its action occurs on boats: on the liner that carries Nya from Beira to Southampton, and in Simon's small boat *Puffin* in Poole harbour, in which he finally departs on a voyage that will take him away from England for three years, giving Nya some time to grow up. At the end of the novel Nya watches the small craft scudding off to sea, and holds 'her breath, daring to hope he would return'. Frank recalls his first reading the book in January 1943 on board a French liner bound for New York, during an uneasy interval when the ship's engines had broken down, and the ship wallowed about in the submarine-infested mid-Atlantic.

Eighteen months later, when hostilities were conclud-ing in Europe but not yet in the Pacific, the carrier on which Frank was serving was dispatched to Sydney, where he spent much of 1945. It's a period which he evidently much enjoyed, but chooses not to describe in his autobiography *Not Entitled*, published fifty years later. 'Of the pleasures of that city I shall not write here, but they were not negligible,' he remarks with classical restraint. Yet the antipodean experience perhaps held an element of romance for Frank, as it clearly did for another young officer in the Royal Navy, the poet Charles Causley, who sailed into Sydney Harbour on HMS *Glory* in 1945 and was deeply moved by the city he encountered. Later back in Cornwall, Causley wrote a poem to 'Celebrate this Southern city/ To which I shall never return', comparing the entire episode of his antipodean journeyings to 'an old forgotten fable', later still – more than thirty years later – Causley did in fact return to Sydney, a city he found greatly transformed but still enduringly fabulous.

Frank himself, back in England, contemplated a return to the antipodes, so it's said, and applied for a lectureship in English at the University of Melbourne. His application was turned down. I asked him once if the story was true, and he smilingly said that it probably was: that he'd put in for a good many jobs at that time and been rejected, 'quite reasonably, in fact, as I didn't have much to show for myself'. Soon of course he did have something to show for himself: an enduring edition of Shakespeare's great play about sea-voyaging (and much besides), *The Tempest*: a play that ends, as romances often do, with the hero sailing back to the land he set off from many years before.

Chief among Frank's pleasures during his wartime stay in Sydney had been the company of poets, and chief among these poets had been A. D. Hope, whose learning, wit and gentleness were greatly to Frank's liking. In 1945 Hope's poems were still unpublished, but circulated in manuscript among his friends and admirers – as they continued to do a decade later, when I first got to know him at Melbourne University, where he was a frequent visitor. He'd been a schoolteacher in New South Wales at the time of Frank's visit, but shifted at the end of that year to the chair of English at Canberra. I'd been lucky enough to inherit that chair in the late Sixties when Alec took early retirement in order to devote himself to full-time writing. He continued to drive every day to the university in a large and battered Holden with a front seat that was so low-slung that he had considerable difficulty in seeing over the dashboard: passing motorists would glimpse only the tufts of silvery hair and a pair of anxious eyes. He was a generous host in the late afternoons, when drink was always available in his room. In the evenings he'd contrive to manoeuvre the big vehicle back across the Commonwealth Bridge at an extremely slow speed, hugging the kerb, and peering learnedly ahead. The local police knew this car and its distinguished owner extremely well, and gave them both a wide berth. At the time of Frank's Canberra visit, Alec occupied an office in a building that had been named after him. Parrots came regularly to his window sill, and poets to his door, and on occasions – by now very hard of hearing – he'd been known to mix them up. ('What do you give them to eat, Alec?' asked one visitor. 'Eat? They don't need to eat at all,' came the reply. 'But they'll drink absolutely anything.') The Humanities Research Centre also occupied the A. D. Hope building, and Frank's office was just a few doors from Alec's. They were soon much in each other's company, recalling earlier times. Whatever happened to Cordukes, the timber merchant with a taste for poetry, who'd originally brought them together? He'd lost his fortune on a cargo of Russian timber, it seemed, which the Sydney dockers had refused to unload, but after that – neither of them seemed to know.

We organised a picnic for the Kermodes in Tidbinbilla,

a large nature reserve an hour or so's drive from Canberra. Grazia had prepared a sumptuous feast. Persian rugs were spread out under the gum trees, with silver and champagne, and the talk and merriment flowed. Anita established close contact with a koala, and sceptically received our opinion that this drowsy animal is habitually stoned on eucalyptus; a theory on which she later sought expert advice, and was able crushingly to refute. A small herd of kangaroos gathered around us, fastidiously preening, delicate noses sniffing the air. 'Clumsy aren't they?' said Grazia, never an uncritical admirer of nature, as they bounded gracefully away. We chorused our raucous agreement.

The first condition of pastoral poetry is that there should be a sharp difference between two ways of life, the rustic and the urban. The city is an artificial product, and the pastoral poet inevitably lives in it, or is the product of its schools and universities. Considerable animosity may exist between the townsman and the countryman.

(Frank Kermode, *English Pastoral Poetry*, 1952)

Finding no countrymen to hand, we did what we could with the kangaroos.

This was the bicentennial year of European settlement in Australia, an event uneasily celebrated throughout the land. Animosities of a more powerful kind erupted. There were sharp and often bitter debates about the legitimacy of the British occupation, about British treatment of Aboriginal people who'd inhabited the country for more than 40,000 years (a figure subsequently extended by new methods of thermoluminescent dating), and about the propriety of celebrating this date at all. Many Aborigines and Aboriginal sympathisers wore black armbands as a sign of contempt. The white celebrators flew their flags proudly claiming their slice of history, and proudly displaying their values. 'Centurial mysticism', Frank had called this phenomenon many years before, and his phrase, like his larger views of history and of value, had a particular resonance in Australia at this dubiously historic moment.

The event which had taken him to St Louis, Missouri, earlier that year (where I suspect the stetsons had been acquired) was another piece of centurial mysticism, the hundredth birthday of T. S. Eliot; an event which he helped to celebrate with a magisterial lecture on Eliot, cities and exile – a lecture later to be repeated to a packed and appreciative Canberra audience. It happened to be a year of centenaries: the two hundredth birthday of Lord Byron, the three hundredth birthday of Thomas Hobbes – not that these events were much noticed in Australia at large, or in Canberra itself, a young city built on ancient Aboriginal settlements, which in 1988 was attempting valiantly to celebrate its own seventy-fifth birthday.And now another birthday is in view, as Sir Frank Kermode is (dizzyingly) five years older than the city of Canberra was at the time of his visit. We wish him a happy birthday and many more years of happy voyaging. In the words of Prospero, 'calm seas and auspicious gales'.

Ian Donaldson

10. THE OPPONENT

T O BEGIN WITH the mean score was about 9–4 in my favour and I always won. Frank held my racquet in his hand admiringly and said, 'It's quite simple, you are a much better player than me.' We met for squash not less than once a week for twenty years. As time passed, the scores got more even and I think Frank sometimes won.

How did I know that Frank wanted to beat me so desperately, seeing that he never revealed his feelings, directly or indirectly in speech? Because his stride became maddeningly jaunty if he won more than two points in succession; because of his firm insistence, so gentle sounding, on the replay of dubious points and balls; because of his solemn, though never emphatic, remonstrance if I screamed 'shit' while the ball was still in play and the point then went my way; because of the way he ruthlessly, joylessly and unerringly killed the loose ball and then put on a smug face. Another thing. If his body happened to get between me and the returning ball he made no attempt to get out of the way. On the contrary, he stood motionless with both elbows protruding rigidly so that collision with him really hurt.

Once I had to lie down in the middle of a game because I was so unfit. The score was 7–4 in Frank's favour. Three minutes later we resumed and I won the next five points, extremely quickly. Frank, who never got sweaty or tired or even out of breath, said very quietly, 'You shouldn't have done that.' I said that I forfeited the game. 'Yes, but it is really a very annoying way to behave,' said Frank, continuing with a monotonous remonstrance and making the emphases, not vocally, but with an up and down sawing movement of his racquet. I said I was sorry but I had to lie down and had given him the game, so would he please now stop chiding. Frank said O.K. he would stop. 'But all the same,' he went on, 'it is a most annoying way to behave.' I didn't hear the end of his sentence because I had left the court in a huff. We made it up under the chestnut trees which shelter King's College School. I said:

> Chestnut candles are lit again
> For the dead that died in the spring
> Dead lovers walk the orchard ways
> And the dead cuckoos sing.

'Housman,' said Frank.
'No,' I said, 'It isn't by Housman.'
'Yes it is,' said Frank. 'Someone else may have written

47

down the words but the poem is by Housman all the same.'

Once I learned the hard way about Frank's forehand drive, when it connected with my balls on its way towards the front wall. I had to lie down for twenty minutes. Frank stood beside me but wasn't very sympathetic.

We never harrowed the squash ground during the precious minutes in the gallery of the King's courts (dusty, cold, littered with broken gear) as we changed our shoes and other stuff. I slowly gathered that he was trying to redesign the English faculty. But this was proving impossible because people were exercising power who should have no right to do so. ('Anita teaches,' he told me, 'and as it happens she teaches very well. But she teaches without anyone knowing that she can teach at all'). And he was being slowly racked by the uniquely Cambridge-flavoured, cold cruelty of the English faculty as they organised themselves against him. I inferred all this very gradually and only by replaying in my mind, and resynthesising over a long period of time, the words he had spoken to me. For there was never a hint of complaint or pain in the tone of voice. Once he said, but with such calm that I neither heard nor understood the words for several days, that he had been walking down the street and suddenly wanted to lie down in it. He resigned his chair in the end of course, just before the lucrative early retirement scheme was introduced. 'You are the only reason for me to remain here,' said Frank in his beautiful, flat way.

We did other things. We drank gin before lunch on Sunday in the conservatory at Luard Road, with Mozart playing on the gramophone. In Michael Jaffe's horrible Red Room, where the fellows of King's congregate at lunch-time in murmuring cliques, we could huddle together safely. I played 'Happy Birthday' to him on the trombone on his sixtieth birthday. And we paid visits to the Royal Box at Covent Garden where we saw *Tristan*

('Love is the same as death') and *Otello*, and where we had parties made boisterous by Tony Tunstall, the naughty principal horn who wouldn't stop drinking and leave for the pit until the lights started to go down. Once Frank came to my house to drive us to the Opera House and drove away again because no one had heard his knock. He thought we had gone without him! Fifteen or perhaps twenty years passed before I took in that Frank really did believe that he had no entitlement to the Regius Chair or to love, honour or respect from his friends, or to anything else at all.

It was natural that Frank should think of me to write about macroeconomics in his Master Guide series as he had no knowledge of the subject himself and I had told him that I was writing a work of genius. I was doing a lot of economic forecasting at the time and it was going well. I said 'in nature's …' but before I could proceed Frank went on '… infinite book of secrecy a little I can read', adding, 'There are two soothsayers in Shakespeare. That's the one from *Antony*.'

Unfortunately my opus needed thirty years' work rather than eighteen months. But Frank got impatient and the subject came up tiresomely at squash. When I said I was contemplating suicide Frank chuckled and said, 'Yes, but finish the book first.' And when, after publication, I said that the book 'divided opinion', thinking of the four professors around the world (one each from Denmark, Italy, the USA and the Irish Republic) whose opinion matched my own, Frank stated flatly that no, opinion about my book was 'universally bad'.

My age approaches Frank's asymptotically, but he still runs and still never gets tired or sweaty. He looks the same as he did twenty-five years ago and still wants to win just as much.

I can't wait for the next game.

Wynne Godley

49

11. SONNET

Where once you were a name on spines of books
Read, marked and learned in duly franker mode,
Of late you are a friend with knowing looks,
Warm heart, wise counsel, welcoming abode.
Together we have stalked the Stratford bard,
Hip-flasked at Highbury, chalked the Savile baize,
Wept at the opera, watched Lara taking guard,
Set towns from Yale to Barga all ablaze.
Your students know the learned, measured sage,
Your readers the insightful polyglot,
I the chimes-at-midnight chum, sans age
And for all time – whose wingèd chariot,
Refusing to believe you're just four score,
Is posting flight-plans for a good few more.

Anthony Holden

12. HANGING ABOUT WITH FRANK

SOME YEARS AGO I mentioned to a young teacher friend of mine in Dorset that I had spent the previous day in London with Frank. He had read Frank's work at university and had been greatly influenced by him. Eager for a glimpse of the great man he asked, 'What did you discuss with him?'

'Oh,' I said, 'we discussed pre-revolutionary Russian writers in relation to the mysticism of Yeats over lunch and in the afternoon we dissected structuralism. We had a little time left over and were going to discuss Pound and Joyce but we decided to have a drink instead.'

He was so impressed I didn't have the heart to disillusion him. Frank and I still have our days in London.

Frank comes down from Cambridge and I travel from Dorset. We meet at his club around twelve, have a drink at the bar and then lunch with a good bottle of wine. After lunch we go down to the basement and get on with the main business of the day – snooker. We usually play quite badly, sometimes very badly. Conversation does take place but not on the rarefied plane my young friend would like to have imagined.

Frank does not sit easily in his club. This slight anxiety about being a member of, or more accurately having access to the portals of, the Establishment springs from his inability to stop himself seeing and appreciating, with some humour, the ludicrousness of his own position within that Establishment. He has a healthy distrust of authority, born perhaps out of his Manx background and reinforced by his time in the Navy.

Our friendship is not based on any shared experience of university or academic life. I left school at fifteen to become a carpenter's apprentice, but I did become a writer and Frank likes and respects writers, while always claiming he himself is not one. Many years ago, after dinner in my house in Fulham, Peter Nicholls and I, full of wine and self-pity, were bemoaning the fact that we had never been to university – never experienced those wonderful three years of freedom where making a living didn't matter and the pursuit of knowledge was all.

Frank got more and more impatient until he could take no more of it. 'You're both talking nonsense,' he exploded. 'You both write and have your work performed. University might well have ruined you. Neither of you has any idea what you are talking about.'

He was right, of course: our vision of university life was hopelessly romantic, and hard as we tried to hang on to our sense of grievance and loss, Frank would have none of it. When he fixes you with that beady eye and asks, 'What exactly do you mean?', you had better get your head together quickly and choose your words carefully.

But he is also the most infinitely courteous man I know, with no sense of the 'I am the great I am', as they say in Ireland. A couple of years ago my daughter rang me to say a cousin of her husband was going to Cambridge for a postgraduate year and could I help him out. I met the young man, a brilliant mathematician, but incredibly shy and diffident. I asked Frank to see him and two days after he arrived Frank gave him tea and an open invitation to come and see him any time. The young man never contacted Frank again, which puzzled and I think slightly hurt Frank because of the discourtesy.

When I next met the young man and asked him why he had behaved so badly, he blushed deeply, stammered an apology and explained what had happened. He had liked Frank enormously, been interested in everything he had said and left determined to keep in touch. When he got back to his college he mentioned he had had tea with Frank and he then learned who Frank was. After that he was terrified of contacting him again because he felt intellectually inadequate. I said, 'But you had already met the man.' He agreed, saying that he had had a wonderful time but only because he had no idea who he was talking to. He'd had the privilege of meeting the real man but the reputation got in the way.

I have sent Frank my work over the years, always with some trepidation because he does not allow friendship to get in the way of an honest and accurate opinion. If he thinks it is inadequate or not up to standard, he says so, and I value his judgement above anybody else's.

I treasure his ability, in conversation, whatever the question or subject, to dredge out of that prodigious memory store the right quote or reference to fine point the discussion or, if memory fails, the immediate leap out of the chair to one of the many bookcases where the fingers walk along the rows until the book is found which will clarify the problem. He always has time and interest if you ring him with a query, and you hear the familiar

'I'll ring you back.' I sit in my study, hundreds of miles away, and I can see the swift movement from room to room until the book is found and then the phone rings and I have my answer.

He is a very private man and adept at hiding his pain. I spent two weeks alone with him in the Spender house in France. It was the time of the break-up with Anita and he was hoping for a letter that would resolve the problem. Every morning he would walk up to the letter box and every morning it was empty. He would stand in his characteristic way, left hand clutching his right arm, right hand holding his pipe which would be puffed at for a minute or two, then the composed walk back to the house.

We both had work to do and at the very beginning we set up a disciplined routine. After breakfast we would retire to different rooms, not to meet again until just before one o'clock. Purely by accident, it seemed, we would bump into each other in the kitchen, having come downstairs to make a cup of coffee. 'How's the work?' 'Oh, fine, fine, must get back as soon as the kettle boils.' Then it would seem rude to walk out and not share the coffee break; then, as we were sitting there anyway, what about one game of cribbage? Now Frank plays this game with a speed and ferocity born of three years of boredom on ships of His Majesty's Navy during the war, and he plays it for a penny a point. He always won the first game, and then I had to get even – which I seldom did. After several games a short walk was advisable to dispel the tension built up in these monumental battles, and then a glass of wine or perhaps a pastis and then, good heavens, it's nearly lunch time.

On one of our walks an incident happened which impressed Frank, and which he still fondly remembers. We were on a narrow track and stepped aside to allow a line of immaculately dressed French riders to go through. As each horse passed, its rider, solemnly and without smiling, raised his hat in thanks. For a courteous man, such dignified courtesy was appropriate.

Frank had driven down in his new Peugeot car, but somehow I did most of the driving. On narrow French hill roads his driving can be somewhat hair-raising. We came out one morning to go shopping and Frank suddenly stopped, demanding the keys and declaring it was his car and he was going to drive. We hadn't gone 200 yards when a French car came from the other direction, not giving an inch, and as it passed it took Frank's driving mirror with it. The Frenchman reversed and he and Frank examined the damage. The Frenchman declared loudly and with good humour that there didn't seem to be much harm done. Diffidently and politely, Frank seemed to agree, and the Frenchman was in his car and away. Back home, the new mirror cost Frank over a hundred pounds; it had been a costly piece of courtesy.

Playing games with Frank is a different matter. Squash, table tennis, cards, he plays to win with a steely determination, but then he is a very determined man. After one of our snooker days I had to leave early, and Frank had two hours to kill before he gave a speech at a dinner. I rang him next morning to see how it had gone and he told me what had happened. He had decided to walk from Mayfair to Bloomsbury. He set off from the club (and anyone who has walked with Frank will know he sets a very fast pace which younger men find hard to match). He had gone half a block when he tripped over a broken paving stone and went sprawling into the road. An approaching truck slammed on its brakes and stopped only yards from his prone figure. Bruised and shaken, he was helped to the pavement where he assured everyone he was fine. I asked whether he'd been to the doctor to have himself checked and, of course, he said no. Frank going to the doctor is a rare event. I asked whether they had been able to get a replacement speaker at such short notice, and he said there was no need as he had gone on to the dinner. Anyone else would have had a stiff drink and gone home.

Over the last few years he has been threatening to ease up, not to do any more lectures abroad, as the travelling is exhausting. Then you get the call that he is off the next day to Milan or New York or Timbuktu. He is indefatigable. Recently, when he was unwell, I went to stay with him, and his main anger was directed at the doctor who told him that it was time to give up playing squash. He has a new doctor now, who has told him that playing squash is extremely good for him. So he is back on court.

Over the years we have shared many family holidays in France and Italy. A ritual developed between us, claimed by Frank to be my doing. It's called a 'sealer'. A glass of whisky before retiring. It is a fine tradition as long as it remains singular. When it becomes plural, the next morning is a little blurred. I look forward to sharing a sealer with my friend Frank for many years to come.

Brian Phelan

13. SIXTY YEARS ON

JUST A BIRTHDAY NOTE (needing only a brief break from EMF and *Alexandria**). It must have been about 1938 – second-year English in Betjeman's admired Liverpool clock tower on Brownlow Hill? – that you had a first 'many happy returns' from me. So some six decades of mixed returns line up behind this latest message, which still manages to keep an eye on EMF's Egyptian years. Even at their remarkable best – and he said as much when writing to Cavafy – he thought peaceful returns were more deeply desired than happy ones.

*E.M. Forster's *Alexandria* is in preparation for the Abinger Edition. Frank is acting as General Editor.

Hardly a reason, all the same, not to wish you more than a bit of both this time.

Insh'Allah, not to mention *mabruk*.

Miriam Allott

14. BEES AND NON-BEING

Consider the following text:

I meet a friend I haven't seen for a long time.

What are you doing now? I ask.

I'm keeping bees.

What sort of bees?

About like this … (he places his hands about a foot apart)

Bees like that? (I place my hands about a foot apart)

Yes. About like that.

What do you keep them in?

I keep them in hives.

What sort of hives?

I keep them in hives like that by about that … (he measures with his hands a space about nine inches by six)

Good heavens. You mean you keep bees like that … (I gesture about a foot between my hands) … in hives like that … (about nine inches by six inches)

Yes, he says. Fuck 'em!

Looking at the narrative above I am more than half (though perhaps less than three-quarters) convinced that its cogency depends in large measure on the tension between its verbal and non-verbal elements.[1] It is

[1] I am influenced, of course, by Dr Clare Bonzine's seminal critical work *Empty Gestures* (Aberdeen University Press, Aberdeen, 1991), which consists of 302 numbered blank pages followed by an

surely central to that tension that the predicament of the bees is never verbalised. They are, to adapt Conan Doyle, the dog that did not bark.[2] Yet, barking or not, the bees remain eloquent. Their very silence is reproach enough; a lesser narrator might have added mimicry to mime (angry buzzing, thorax-scratching, etc), which would inevitably have masked the simple mimesis of this specific abuse of beedom.

There is further use of verbal absence. In the coda – 'Fuck 'em' – notice the absence of the first two letters of the word 'them'. It is surely no accident[3] that in the Greek alphabet the symbol for the letter 'th' is a lozenge with a horizontal stripe. In other words (or absence of them), a bee symbol. In accordance with natural justice the bee has (almost) the last word, or, in this case, non-word. A reference, surely, to the tacit recognition by humans that bees, by accident or design, so far lack the power of speech or language.[4]

---

extensive index and bibliography. Incidentally, there is an entry for Bees in the index which refers the reader to page 181 *passim*.

2 The whole question of the fauna of the Holmes canon, and in particular the incidence of dogs and bees, is most fruitfully explored in Clare da Silva's *The Question of Fauna in the Holmes Canon* (Alabama University Press, Alabama, 1982). It was this essay which first established that the first notebook sketch of 'The Hound of the Baskervilles' was entitled 'The Bee of the Baskervilles'. Professor da Silva also points to Conan Doyle's lifelong preoccupation with the insect by revealing that 'The Speckled Band' started life as 'The Bandled Speck'.

3 For a discussion of the accidental in the birth of literature, see 'I was the Porlock Postman', letter to the *Western Daily Press*, 9 July 1824, by Enoch Jakeways.

4 I am indebted for much of this discussion of lacunae within words to Dr Clare Grigson-Speake's notion of the 'missing signifiers' which she observed in the labelling of vegetables by greengrocers in the county of Essex (UK). She was perhaps the first to record the importance of parsnips being described by their retailers

Similarly,[5] the motif recurs as the fulcrum of Ronald Lavatory's great novel of frustrated hope and disappointed love, *The Empty Hive* (Methuen, London, 1931). The passage repays quoting in full. It is the moment when the hero, significantly named Ronald Lavatory, leaves his cottage on the Sussex Downs one morning.

Ronald closed the cottage door behind him. The weather had fulfilled its dawn promise and a warm breeze wafted from the sea. Just beyond the garden gate Ronald noticed a winged insect, with black and yellow stripes, flying in the general direction of Plumpton racecourse. He followed it for miles, hoping against hope that it would lead him to a treasure-trove of golden honey. But, alas, it was not a bee.

The emptying of the literary cliché is complete. The almost literal defenestration of everything Lavatory stands for (through the window of irony, the round window) changes everything, and forever. Is the bee not a bee? No. And that is not the question. It is overwhelmingly[6] the answer.

Of course, it is but a short step from Ronald Lavatory

as 'nips'. The missing signifier here, of course, is 'pars'. As she puts it (*Gender Studies among the Brassica Family*, Chelmsford University Press, 1978): 'The mind cruises around the frustrated expectation of the first syllable, licking delicately away at the (now supplied) "pars". The skin, as it were, of the syllable once rasped away, the ironic fruit is revealed. "Pars" = "Père" = Pater = "Pa". The absent father, leaving his abandoned "nips" = nippers – children in Essex parlance. A whole Strindbergian drama enacted on a simple greengrocer's label.' Dr Grigson-Speake is equally revealing with cauliflowers. It was something of a shock to discover that Wavell's celebrated anthology of poetry was intended to be entitled 'Other Men's Cauliflowers'.

5 'Similarly' in the sense that 'similarly' is a useful word with which to start a new paragraph. See Prof. Clare Dexville's *Checklist of Critical Adverbs* (Nairobi Higher Education Authority, Nairobi, 1926).

6 For 'overwhelmingly', see above.

to Marcel Proust.[7] It is one of the enduring mysteries of the Modernist tradition that in all twelve volumes of the Scott Moncrieff translation there are only nineteen references to bees. (And one could hardly accuse Moncrieff of a less than perfect knowledge of the French word for 'bee' when he saw it in Proust's text.)

Indeed, one might say that it is the very absence of bees which hovers, one might almost say buzzes around *A la recherche du temps perdu*. Think of the hawthorn blossoms of the Guermantes Way. Think of the endless pages of description of their scent, their colour, their similarity to young girls dancing in the moonlight. And yet ... (and might not 'and yet' stand as an epigram for the whole novel?) ... and yet in all these flowery pages there is not one reference to the means by which the hawthorn blossoms are pollinated year after year. For what else might be responsible but the bee?[8] What is Proust trying to tell us here? Surely[9] that the bee-mute glade of the hawthorns is a perfect mirror of homosexual love which the artifice of Albertine is so at pains to obscure. Or over which that perfect mirror Proust is at such pains to cloud.[10] The equation seems to be: no bee:

7 I take some issue with Clare Isinglass in her *From Proust to Lavatory: The Yellow Brick Road* (Faber & Faber, London, 1990). Proust's death and Lavatory's commitments at his prep school during the First World War would, and indeed should, have precluded the sexual liaison which is at the heart of her hypothesis.

8 On my suggestion one of my postgraduate students, Ms Clare Trogir-Syvabo, spent some weeks during January and February 1995 trying to pollinate hawthorns in the Illiers (Combray) district of north-west France with a number of rabbit tails. The results were not encouraging. Another triumph, perhaps, of bee over rabbit?

9 See above, *Checklist of Critical Adverbs*, ibid.

10 I am grateful to Dr Clare Nantwich for her article 'Grammar – Whom Gives a Shit?' (London Review of Books, vol xxxi no. 3, 1994, pp. 103-117.)

yes, homosexual promiscuity. And indeed (if indeed in the sense of in-deed is appropriate here), if the young Proust (if indeed, in both senses, it is he) is de facto the absent bee, as he well may be, he must surely be both witness to the apparent virgin birth of the hawthorn blossom and narrator of its subsequent lack of progeny. This is the paradox. Or one of them, anyway. If there are, as there probably are, more of them.

Perhaps Proust had in mind the lines from Euripides:

> Love is a bee in the garden of the world
> And for the flowers there is poison in his breath.

More than perhaps. The whole novel shouts the fact that he must have.[11]

Or – and I admit it is a big or – it is equally probable that during his long, hot summers at Combray the young Marcel had access to hot, dusty attics in which, in old tin trunks, were stored the friable uniforms of soldiers of the Napoleonic campaigns. Friable but for the buttons, each stamped with the Emperor's personal symbol. Yes, the bee.

In the light of this[12] it is tempting to see the whole novel as an elegiac farewell to Empire. (The French Empire.) Indeed, if I were asked tomorrow to prepare a new translation of Proust (o181-994 1992) I would call it *Remembering the Bee. When it was about. Which wasn't often.*

Anyway, that's enough of that.

John Fortune

---

11 An interesting experiment in shouting the whole of *A la recherche du temps perdu* from a Scottish clifftop was carried out under my direction at a three-week seminar at the Callanish stone circle on the Isle of Lewis in the late summer of 1987. The girls performed magnificently.

12 Cynics might say 'In the light of what?', to which I would respond that the Owl of Minerva flies at night.

3

MAGAZINES, LONDON

AND SOME ACADEMIC FLAK

---

15. JOHN SUTHERLAND

16. MARY-KAY WILMERS

17. NOEL ANNAN

18. KARL MILLER

19. PETER PORTER

20. CHARLES OSBORNE

21. STEPHEN FENDER

22. RICHARD POIRIER

photo: Mark Kermode

15. FASHIONING A SYLLABUS

MY FIRST SIGHT of J. F. Kermode was at Manchester, in 1964 (as I calculate). I had a friend – since died – who had landed a three-year 'temporary' lectureship in the English department. 'That's Kermode,' he hissed, as we sat in the common room, misaccenting the name as people routinely did, 'Kerm*ode*'. Bill, my friend, didn't like J. F. K. Why? Because he was writing 'clever-clever' things for the *Manchester Guardian* (as it then was). I went away and read some of those clever-clever things in *Puzzles and Epiphanies* and liked them a lot (particularly, I recall, the essay on Graham Greene's recent *A Burnt-out Case*. The admiration was tinged with that aching sense, familiar to academics, that I could never do anything as good myself even if I lived to be forty.

A little later someone passed on to me a donnish and not very funny joke (are there any others?) about there having been a lot of bedroom crockery at Newcastle in the late 1940s, what with Ure (ewer) and Kermode (commode) in the same department. The quip stuck in my mind while a million more important things have been lost.

My next sighting was at Edinburgh, in 1966. It was around the time that Frank was trying out versions of the lectures that subsequently became *The Sense of an Ending*. It is one of the paradoxes of Kermode that what at the time seems incredibly complicated becomes crystal clear over the years. When I heard that lecture, on the seventh floor of the David Hume Tower, I was completely flummoxed. When I most recently revisited *The Sense of an Ending*, it seemed as direct and comprehensible as Hume himself. It's taken me three decades, but I've finally caught up with J. F. Kermode, 1966.

At the reception after the lecture Frank was casually

brilliant in conversation. The younger academics were arrayed around him like iron filings round a magnet. As we left the New Town flat my friend (and Frank's former PhD student, Stephen Fender) muttered, 'My God, he makes you feel like a shrimp.' I demurred, but in my shrimp-soul knew he was right.

When he took over at UCL in 1967, Frank was obliged to undertake a massive reorganisation (the Augean condition of the department is comically immortalised in David Lodge's *The British Museum is Falling Down*, published – at some risk of libel action, one would have thought – two years before). As part of the operation Frank systematically raided Edinburgh. Three members of its English department, Steve Fender, Michael Mason and myself, were brought down over the three years, 1969–72, caught in Kermode's shrimping net. Fender was particularly important in the founding of an American literature specialism at London University – an innovation regarded at the time as revolutionary.

I was the last of the trio to arrive. 1972 was an exciting time to be working in English studies (the only exciting time during my lifetime, I now think). Kermode had shot through the provincial universities of England like Cromwell in Marvell's poem. At UCL, however, he seemed to have found a resting place. In *Not Entitled* he says that this, if anywhere, was his happiest academic berth. Despite the bruising business of the resignation from *Encounter* in 1967 he evidently relished metropolitan life.

Noel Annan, the Provost, had the eccentric (as it now seems) theory that the English department was the heart of any great university. He gave Kermode a free hand and generous resources. Frank used part of them to secure a chair for his fellow *Encounter* rebel, Stephen Spender. Professor Spender did not have a first degree, let alone a PhD. As a colleague he was a source of unprofessional delight. At one staff meeting, where a student's progress was being discussed (one of Spender's tutees, as it happened), he musingly reported: 'I remember nothing about her, except that after she leaves the room, there is a lingering fragrance of roses.'

Frank was happy, and everyone at UCL was happy. He had as his co-chair Randolph Quirk, with whom he had been at school – a Manx gang of two. *Soixante-huitards* both, they seceded from London University. The English department at UCL went 'college based', as the jargon was. Kermode and Quirk liberated their colleagues' teaching from the University syllabus and (even more liberatingly) from its stifling Senate House examination bureaucracy. What Frank discovered, to his delight evidently, was that he had autonomous power (the kind of dictatorial power abused by some of his predecessors) to fashion a syllabus in his own intellectual image. He was master in his own department.

He and Quirk went about their task methodically. After the declaration of independence came a new constitution. A departmental board of studies was set up, in which the head of department and other professors were simply *inter pares*. Through this machinery the New Syllabus was delivered. It was, despite the democratic machinery, very much the offspring of Kermode's brain, sold to the department by his personal conviction that it would work.

As outlined in the famous 'underground map', the syllabus had three nuclei: Renaissance Literature (specifically Donne's longer poetry, *The Faerie Queene*, and *Paradise Lost*), Shakespeare, and Chaucer. The demand on the undergraduate was uncompromising: *all* of Spenser's and Milton's epics, Shakespeare's drama, and Chaucer's poems. No smorgasbord or picknicking.

Anyone who has worked in academic life knows the sterile oppositions of breadth and depth, of field coverage and textual analysis, of literary history and genre. The foundations of the Kermodian new syllabus rested

65

on a belief that certain difficult core texts must be mastered. And this belief rested on a basic conviction that literary criticism is a set of learned techniques – something that Frank occasionally likened to skill in professional sport (this belief in cumulatively acquired skills accounts for the persistence of final examinations at UCL, while most of the British system has opted for continuous assessment and modularity).

There were no set readings or staff solutions. Texts were, in Frank's memorable term, 'patient'. They could absorb any number of interpretations. This keyed into what was then an unusual feature at UCL and is now virtually unique, the one-to-one tutorial. Dialogue – not classroom discussion – was the department's principal educational discourse.

Lying outside the prescribed nuclei were a range of options which could only be reached through 'gateways' ('American', for example, could only be arrived at via 'Romantics'). The aim was to allow the undergraduate to assemble a course of study with whatever inflection she or he preferred (medieval, 'language', modern) but to contain it within a firm but flexible architecture. It proved an extraordinarily durable model. With certain erosions (students, regrettably, no longer come up able to take on Spenser and Milton whole) the New Syllabus is still in place. It is one of Kermode's monuments.

Meanwhile, at the cutting edge of the subject, Frank was running the pioneering graduate seminars which transfused theory into the torpid English academic system. Luminaries like Roland Barthes found themselves in the unlikely setting of Foster Court. Barthes, with his love of elegant artifice, would have been delighted to know that it was, in fact, a perfect simulacrum of Foster Court. The original building (a mattress warehouse, belonging to Maples on Tottenham Court Road) had burned down in the 1950s. The insurance company insisted that the building be faithfully reconstructed in all its mattress-warehouse unloveliness – doubtless to discourage any prospective academic arsonist with architectural renewal on his mind. Like the Kermodian syllabus, Foster Court endures.

Entrance to Frank's graduate seminar was by his invitation. I was invited but by 1972 it had been going three years. It was like trying to get on a train travelling at fifty miles an hour. About five years later I was in a position to profit, but by then it was all over. I was flattered to have been a spectator. If I'd arrived at UCL three years earlier, I suspect the shape of my subsequent career would have been different.

Frank didn't last long at Foster Court, although his effect is still visible and palpable. By 1974 he had moved on to Cambridge. His career has any number of highpoints. I like to think, chauvinistically, that UCL was one of them. He had arrived at an unusually propitious moment. The department was ripe for reform. English studies was revered as it no longer is and the 1960s were hospitable to new thinking. Kermode had established himself as the most powerful critic of his generation, and the peculiarly autocratic nature of the department put levers in his hand. This combination of elements allowed him to express himself as an educationist (a word, I suspect, he would not like). Generations of students and their teachers have benefited and still do.

John Sutherland

16. FRANK AND THE LONDON REVIEW OF BOOKS

THE *London Review of Books* owes its existence to Frank Kermode. In January 1979 the Thomson Organisation, hapless and unhappy Canadian proprietors of *The Times* and its satellites, made a final attempt to get the better of the UK print unions by not publishing their newspapers. When, six months later, there was still no agreement and *The Genesis of Secrecy* was about to come out, Harvard University Press, the book's publishers, were wondering how, in the absence of the *TLS*, they could alert the world to its existence. Frank himself was untroubled at the thought of his book not being reviewed. 'Unlike most authors I find that the date of publication invariably coincides with the moment when my loathing for my book reaches its maximum intensity,' he wrote in the *Observer* on 10 June, a week before publication was due. The doleful note wasn't new: as his friends and readers know, it is almost always present when Frank writes about himself. In fact, he went on to say, he would prefer it if his books were ignored, though he knew that 'real writers' feel differently about these things.

So it was on behalf of 'real writers' and their readers that he went on to lament the absence of the *TLS* and to cite the example of the *New York Review of Books*, which had come into existence when the *New York Times* was on strike. Why, he asked, could something similar not be done here? Why had the possibility of creating a new literary paper not even, as far as he knew, been considered? Lack of money? Or, more plausibly, lack of energy and imagination? Whatever the reason or excuse, no sooner had Frank said that he found 'the lapse of six months without the slightest visible stir of enterprise very depressing' than plans were drawn up for three new literary journals.

At the end of September the three new papers – the *Literary Review*, *Quarto* and the *LRB* – each produced their first issue. But by then the Thomson outfit was in the process of selling its papers to Rupert Murdoch and before the *London Review*'s second issue was out the *TLS* was back in the shops. The first issue of the *LRB*, published 'marsupially' (as Karl Miller described it) inside the *New York Review*, had sold 18,000 copies. The return of the *TLS* put us in our place (or what many people considered to be our place); sales plummeted; advertising disappeared; and we separated, not entirely amicably, from the *New York Review*. The contributors, however, kept their nerve – not that we ever told them the whole truth – and a decade or so later, we got back to where we'd been at the start.

Twenty years on, *Quarto* has disappeared but the *Literary Review* continues in its amiable, upper-class way, while the *LRB* has all but caught up with the *TLS*. Frank may sound dejected when he speaks on his own account: it takes unusual authority to bring three papers into the world by snapping your fingers.

Frank's contribution to the *LRB* goes way beyond his maieutic role, however. He has written more pieces for the paper than anyone else and no one has written better pieces than he has. In the past few weeks I have reread maybe a hundred of them – say, half of those he has written over the years – and I am both stunned by how good they are and appalled to think how much I fail to take in as I sit at my desk on an ordinary editorial day, worrying about spacing and hyphenation. I read them in no particular order, going backwards and forwards between the late Nineties and the early Eighties, making a note of thoughts and turns of phrase that I'd like to remember.

The first piece I reread, published in March 1989, was about Paul de Man, 'the great impresario of the rhetorical impasse', as Frank describes him. I remembered the article reasonably well ('reasonably well' is the best my memory can do) but wanted to read it again because it's such a good (and, in my eyes, sympathetic) example of the ingenuity of thought and generosity of outlook that are among the strongest reasons for admiring what Frank writes. A volume of the young de Man's wartime journalism – collaborationist, anti-semitic – had been published in translation towards the end of the previous year, and the enemies of literary theory, backed by the press, were having a great time making connections between deconstruction and de Man's hidden past, while his friends and disciples cast about for plausible ways to defend him. True to his conciliatory habits, Frank follows de Man's career from young Belgian journalist in the early years of the German occupation to charismatic Yale professor, neither condemning nor endorsing, but leaving you with the feeling that the issues involved could not have been more thoroughly or fairly set out. But what makes the piece especially sympathetic is a kind of wisdom (I suppose that's what it is) that comes with the ability to take into account the circumstances of someone else's life, however alien, and to do it without making a meal of the whole business. In this instance he is led to turn the tables first on one camp:

One wonders whether, had the Germans occupied Britain at the end of 1940, there would have been no clever young people willing to say in collaborationist newspapers (and wouldn't there have been collaborationist newspapers?) that this was at least not altogether a bad thing

then on the other:

although defences of de Man are decently animated by affection for a dead and admired friend, these attempts at biographical exculpation, these rakings through his evolving, exacting, rather melancholy writings, often seem to lack any serious understanding of how even people of high intelligence are sometimes induced to behave, especially when they may be under stress of a kind the exculpators have the good fortune to know nothing about.

Equally likeable, even admirable, is the ironic note on which the piece ends. 'The insiders,' Frank writes, should now be happy to stop worrying about de Man's 'youthful errors' and – this is the really appealing bit – 'get on with their necessary and impossible projects'.

If I go on much longer Frank is going to wish I'd never been asked to contribute to this book, but it just is the case that there are very few – if any – academics who are interested in so many things and able to write about them with so much authority. Frank has written in the *LRB* (and, regrettably, elsewhere) about music and painting and philosophy, about history and politics, about contemporary novels and poetry, even, latterly (in the *New York Times*), about Princess Diana, as well as on the subjects one would expect him to write on. Another piece I remembered liking especially, and wanted to reread, was about Howard Hodgkin and the 'honoured place' of the 'leg-pull' in modern art – 'the biggest' of which, Frank wrote, is 'to kid us into believing that words can be found to explain the beauty of these patches of paint'.

I see now that a majority of the sentences I was keen to remember have to do with the difficulty and/or impossibility of knowing what to say and how to say it – David Sylvester, to take another example, has an 'almost unrivalled power to gaze and to find language to express the rewards of intensive contemplation' – but that is to do with me, not with Frank, who always gives the impression of being perfectly at ease at his typewriter, in command of his thoughts and his words, whether he's writing about smells or about Shakespeare, a book he detests or one he admires, and does so without ever tumbling into culpable ease. 'A good review,' he said in 1987, in a review of two collections of reviews, 'gives a fair account of the book yet is a well-composed piece in its own right ... its purpose is not to remind the reader that the reviewer is cleverer and more interesting than the book under consideration'. But sometimes a reviewer, whatever his intentions, can't help showing that he's a more attentive, more interesting and wiser reader – as well as being funnier and a lot more stylish – than the author of the book he is writing about.

Mary-Kay Wilmers

17. REINVIGORATING UCL

I DON'T THINK I ever met Frank until he came to University College, London, but when I was Provost of King's, Cambridge I often heard his name. Half a dozen or more of the dons in the faculty of English were close friends, and reading literary criticism was a hobby of mine. They spoke of him as the brightest of the younger generation of critics and it struck me how each of them praised something he had written in his own field of study. So when James Sutherland retired from his professorship, his name was in my mind, and when I was asked to write in this book I thought I might set down what I remember of his advent and departure from London.

The department of English at UCL was ruled by a double-headed eagle. There was the Northcliffe Professor of Modern English Literature and the Quain Professor of Medieval and Linguistic Studies. The usual committee was set up to discuss the names of a possible successor to Sutherland, and naturally the Quain Professor, Hugh Smith, was a member of the committee. The difficulty, I realised only too well, was not in assembling a collection of suitable candidates. It was in dealing with Professor Smith.

Smith's subject was not Anglo-Saxon nor linguistics. He was an authority on English place names – hardly a subject that took a central place in English studies. Smith was a bully and held tyrannical sway over the graduate students and members of the department who studied language. They were invited to attend his seminar. The seminar was held in the Marlborough Arms, a pub next to the college. Everyone attending was expected to drink pint after pint of beer while Smith held forth slandering every person and institution that came into his mind. His coat and trousers were beer-stained and sweaty, his language was as filthy as his clothes, and the conclusion of his diatribe was that no scholar was as learned as he was.

As the prospects of promotion for the lecturers, and the success of the graduate students in obtaining a PhD, depended on Smith, the atmosphere stank not only of beer but of sycophancy. He kept the graduate students on tenterhooks by hinting every so often that he was thinking of appointing someone in their field of study – and then again implying that perhaps he had other plans in mind. The junior lecturers were there to fetch and carry for him. One day he forgot his keys and sent one of them all the way to his home in Gloucestershire to fetch them.

When UCL was founded in 1828, it had to endure the sneers of Oxford and Cambridge that its students were not required to know Latin and Greek. Its founders proved their academic respectability by insisting that students who studied languages must master philology – in the case of English that meant learning Anglo-Saxon, Old and Middle English. After that one studied the history of literature. The question, why does this poem move us, and why do other poems of different styles and techniques also move us – in other words literary criticism – was anathema to the professors of English who suspected that to study that would lead to soulful essays on Shelley. W. P. Ker denounced literary criticism as so much 'chatter about Harriet'. This tradition had been carried on by James Sutherland with his splendid edition of Pope. Smith was violently opposed to literary criticism, particularly of the kind that had developed in Cambridge under the influence of I. A. Richards, F. R. Leavis and William Empson. At the very first meeting of the committee he announced that anyone whom the committee wanted to put before the university's appointments committee must be acceptable to him, someone whom he felt he could work with; and he insisted that one of the names to be put forward must be that of

73

Arthur Brown, his colleague in the department.

Brown was the leading Smith sycophant, a ginger-haired red-faced lecturer, engaged in textual scholarship. One of his graduate students wrote a searing account of being under his supervision. Every square foot of his room was filled with piles of books and papers, card indexes and memoranda, a chaos in which the theses of aspiring graduate students sank, submerged for months. He would return to his room after the seminar over lunch at the Marlborough Arms drunk, shout abuse at some inoffensive colleague, and descend into sleep. He rarely made a helpful comment on the progress of his student's thesis, probably because he had never read it. This was the man Smith proposed to run as his candidate for the Northcliffe chair. He found no supporters on the committee. One name, however, stood out among the rest: Frank Kermode. Although Kermode was already well known as a literary critic, Smith could hardly deny that Frank had written an erudite work on Milton. Moreover, Frank had served his apprenticeship engaged on the sort of scholarship Smith approved of, in his case editing an unfinished epic of Abraham Cowley and collaborating at Reading with D. J. Gordon on a long article and on elucidating a Ben Jonson masque. With an ill grace Smith conceded that he might be able to work with him.

Perhaps the most important task of any vice-chancellor or principal is to induce men and women of distinction, the best in the field, to apply for a professorship in his institution. He must know something about the best men and women in every subject, or at least know whom to consult clandestinely. I had already picked Frank in my mind. He had a reputation for invigorating departments of which he was head: he had done so at Reading and again at Manchester. My worry was that he had recently moved to Bristol, but I hoped that the lure of London literary life as well as the distinction of UCL in other fields might induce him to move. Much to my relief he indicated informally that if offered the chair he would accept. The external referees appointed by the university agreed. And then came a piece of singular good fortune. Before Frank arrived to take up the post Professor Smith died. When Randolph Quirk was elected to Smith's chair, Brown realised that his last hope of promotion had vanished and he left the country for Australia.

The head of a department in the older civic universities had considerable power. He could appoint to vacant posts virtually whomever he thought fit. Recommendations for promotion to a readership or senior lectureship were in his hands and he could put his stamp on the place. Frank was helped by the fact that Smith's successor, Randolph Quirk, was like himself a Manxman and entirely sympathetic to what Frank was doing, as well as to reviving interest in the way the English language was developing. In his autobiography Frank has described his time at University College which he clearly enjoyed. He was an admirable chairman of the department and although there were some of the old guard left who disapproved of the changes he made, the rest of the members of the department were delighted. He opened up the department to the wider world. He encouraged by his own example the practice of literary criticism, wrote reviews for the weeklies, as well as publishing books – perhaps the text of some prestigious set of lectures he had been invited to give in America.

It was characteristic of his tact and good manners that he came to me to ask how I would react if he put forward the name of Stephen Spender to join the department as a professor. He foresaw that there might be snide comments in the press and criticism in the university if someone outside the academic profession was appointed in this way and that I might be embarrassed. I had always heard that Spender was a fine teacher with a reputation as such in the United States where he had moved from university to university, and I told Frank to go ahead. (Later Frank's successor, Karl Miller, brought in the South African novelist, Dan Jacobson, a no less successful appointment). Nor were these the only appointments from the world of letters. A. S. Byatt came and so did a poet, Grey Ruthven, better known later as Lord Gowrie, a future minister for the arts under Margaret Thatcher.

Meanwhile in the Seventies another method of treating literature appeared. Frank invited the French sage Roland Barthes to the department, and he immersed himself in structuralism, in the work of Lacan, Derrida and Foucault. He emerged the other end convinced that this tree bore Dead Sea fruit. At any rate, members of the department knew what deconstruction was about.

In those days the leading departments in the humanities were Classics, Geography and Philosophy. English now rose to join them. After Smith's gloomy reign, Frank enlivened the department. His warm, friendly, sunny face welcomed experiment, novelty, initiatives. It was like a sunrise. The pernickety was succeeded by the excitement of general ideas. Frank's criticism was never flabby. Indeed in exchanges with other scholars who challenged him it could be sharp and biting. But his natural bent was warm, interested, alert. He and Randolph Quirk transformed the department so that it regained the status that it enjoyed before the two world wars by doing something different from the days of Ker and Chambers.

And then one day Frank called on me to say that he had been offered the King Edward VII chair in English at Cambridge and was minded to accept. I remonstrated with him. Did he realise that he would suffer a considerable drop in salary as I had placed him at the very top of the scale for humanities professors? He said he could probably meet the shortfall by doing more writing. Did he know what the faculty of English at Cambridge was like? By then the most vituperative and impossibly difficult colleague, F. R. Leavis, had retired but, if there were few Leavisites in the department, there was a considerable number of prima donnas, men and women who had a just estimate of their own importance in literary studies. Like Naaman, the Syrian, they considered Abana and Pharpar better than all the waters of London. Why had this outsider been foisted on Cambridge by the electors to the chair? His position in Cambridge would be entirely different from that at UCL. Here he was master of the department, could make, subject to agreement with Randolph, virtually whatever appointments he pleased. He had been able to transform the department by using those qualities of tact and leadership which had been among the many reasons why he had been so successful in reviving literary studies in the civic universities.

I went on to say that he might think that the Regius Chair (for that in effect was what the King Edward VII chair was) was of such prestige that he would be accepted as *primus inter pares*. He would be wrong. The fact that he would hold the most prestigious chair would carry no sort of acceptance of his leadership. It would not even carry the chairmanship of the faculty board. The faculty of English had been run, if that was the word, by a number of elder statesmen who managed somehow to compose the rivalries within the faculty, possibly because most of the members of the staff had either grown up with them or had actually been taught by them. They had now retired. The present holder of the chair, L. C. Knights, at one time a contributor to Leavis's *Scrutiny*, was disillusioned and had made no impact. He was later to recall how at his first meeting of the faculty board, 'Voices were raised, the table was thumped and Drs X and Y mutually demanded apologies from each other.' We talked about the state of the department in my time: I had served on its appointments committee as an outside referee for a few years. But I spoke in vain. Frank seemed convinced that what he had achieved at Manchester he could bring about at Cambridge. After all, he had been recognised in this appointment as the head of his profession. Who could blame him for moving? I did, however, tell him that if he decided to go, I would do my best to get King's College, where I had been Provost before I moved to London, to elect him to a fellowship.

Frank himself has given an entertaining account of the reasons why he resigned from the King Edward VII chair after a splendid row over an appointment in which he considered that a junior lecturer had been unjustly treated. But the truth was that he was never happy there and few, except in his own college, extended a hand of friendship to him. Yet it is to Cambridge that he has retired, and there to my delight I meet him even if, as is all too often, it is at the memorial service for some friend and scholar of days gone by. I hear myself saying like Justice Shallow, 'And is old Double dead?' But avaunt! such melancholy thoughts. I welcome Frank to the lists of us octogenarians, the finest literary critic of his generation.

Noel Annan

18. THE LITERARY JOURNALIST

M Y FRIENDSHIP with Frank Kermode goes back a long way, and I shall write here about the early years of my connection with this shaman of beginnings, middles and ends. We worked together in literary journalism for four decades. The collaboration began in 1958, soon after I went to the *Spectator* as its literary editor. He was then an assistant lecturer at Reading University, as I remember – though it may be that the self-deprecations of his memoir *Not Entitled* ('at the outset quite unfitted' for the job at Manchester that followed the one at Reading) have caused me to demote him.

At the *Spectator* he was rapidly, not to say immediately, promoted to regular appearances. His first piece was a subtle one on C. P. Snow's novel *The Conscience of the Rich*, a slice of Snow's Lewis Eliot sequence; in this instalment, he wrote, Eliot witnesses 'another tragedy of possessive love', and the renunciation of power, once more, by men who love it. There's 'an effect of déjà vu not unfamiliar to this novelist's readers'. His second piece, a fortnight later, was on a novel which he spoke of, in the very narrow compass afforded him, as a masterpiece, a great book: this was the eighteenth-century Chinese *Dream of the Red Chamber* ('achieves a high civility without sacrificing nature'). It was already clear that while Frank was a known Romanticist and Shakespearian he was by no means a specialist. He was a scholar of wide range, who could sometimes be guarded but was unlikely to display much of the timidity he later suspected of himself in his memoir.

The relevant back-numbers of the paper shed light on his critical debut. The paper had been running for some while as a radical Tory sheet, hospitable to the Gaitskellite Left and to the Movement school of writers led by Kingsley Amis and Philip Larkin. My plan was to build on what there was at the back with contributions from *Scrutiny* veterans and other Leavis sympathisers – among them, D. W. Harding. Harding's account of James Gould Cozzens's novel *By Love Possessed* – the work of an American writer previously and subsequently neglected, by and large, on both sides of the Atlantic – was experienced (by me) as a flying start to my editorial tenure. This piece on 'a major figure among serious novelists' was entitled 'The Limits of Conscience'. Conscience was something of a preoccupation of the time, or of one part of the time, as were seriousness and sensibility. It was, in part, an age of feeling.

Frank Kermode was more than fit to flourish in this distinctly miscellaneous and intellectually divided company, but it may not have been initially obvious to his

79

readers and watchers just where he fitted in. There would have been those who reckoned that he was too academic for literary journalism, and some of the more entrenched practitioners in Leavis's abhorred 'London literary world' may have seen him as a threat. Others may have felt that he was insufficiently moralistic in the style that had emerged from Cambridge. But he had his own way of being judicial. The verdicts of this student of the High Modernist masters were far from unfavourable to the novels of Amis and the poetry of Larkin, and there were Londoners of the time by whom all three could be seen as provincials. If he could be more taxing than many reviewers he was also more rewarding and more idiosyncratic. He referred early on to James Joyce's interest in the Renaissance mage Giordano Bruno (born in Nola, and known to Joyce as 'the Nolan') as being an interest so keen that at the age of eighteen he took the stage name of Gordon Brown, which has lately become rather more of a name to conjure with than it was then. It's hard to say, of Kermode and Joyce, which was the more Nostradamus on this occasion.

These back-numbers reveal that there was a war being waged in London between critics and scholars, on the one hand, and journalists on the other, with both sides at it on the paper. Critics were prone to severities and misgivings. In reviewing a book on modern British and American poets, Harding mentioned a failure, at times, to make 'called-for adverse comment'. Not long afterwards, Frank's friend John Wain, a very good critic and a very good journalist, and a supportive admonisher, as I can attest, of newcomers to the profession, published a poem entitled 'On Being insulted by a Popular Journalist', which appeared on the same page as a review by Alan Brien of Kenneth Allsop's book on the current literary scene, *The Angry Decade*. Alan spoke up for his friend's book, while remarking that he'd been 'passionately unfair' to Wain, whose poem, in 'Excelsior' mode, concludes:

> But patience: those who climb the path
> To where those fruits and flowers grow
> Which I have travelled far to seek
> May never halt or swerve for wrath:
> Muse, is it not a boast to show
> His spittle hanging from my cheek?

Kenneth Allsop wrote a letter in the following number smiling at this 'splendid paranoiac poem'. Looking back at the poem in something other than the anger alleged of the period, I have a little trouble in thinking it a laughing matter. There was pain and insult on both sides: but journalists were better able than critics to summon a smile in the course of such exchanges.

All scenes are tormented and divided, literary scenes more than most; and this one was more tormented and divided than most literary scenes. Alan Brien noted on this occasion that 'journalist' had become a dirty word in intellectual circles: the journalist was being demonised as 'a smart, superficial wordmonger who wears a veneer of education as a prostitute wears a mask of make-up, who would rather make a pun than a point, and rather hit a headline than study a footnote'. There's a touch here of a paranoia of the opposing side – the popular side. But Alan was quite right: the word was a reproach in certain circles. It has yet to become an honorific.

In the same issue as the poem, W. W. Robson, scholar and critic, expressed 'misgivings' about classical American literature and the 'imaginative thinness' of Hawthorne and Melville, 'the least secure of great novelists'. In the previous issue, defending himself against Graham Greene in a letter to the paper, Randolph Churchill had owned up, on one of the few occasions when he could be considered disarming, to the thinness of his own imagination.

I recall a remark of Robson's which belongs to the late

Fifties or not long after, to a time when critics would refer to each other as Mr This or Dr That, and a decorum of impersonality was observed or deferred to. He had run through a Third Programme script of his in rehearsal when the producer entered the studio to offer his congratulations. There was just one small thing, enthused the producer. Could one or two of those sentences which began with 'One feels' or 'One is forced to the conclusion' be altered to 'I feel' or 'I think'? Wallace Robson demurred. He had misgivings. 'I don't want to sound like John Wain.' This was a joke, let it be said, and I don't want it to sound as if Wallace was being nasty about John, who I think, or feel, was his friend. But there can be no doubt that he preferred to say 'one'.

So the journalists wore their smiles and their masks, while scholar critics made their limiting judgements. They did not get on, except that in a sense they did. Critic and journalist could be the one person, and the volume of recruits from the universities to the profession that contained them both had increased, to the distress of Evelyn Waugh. Frank was not above the battle I am remembering, which accompanied the process of assimilation in which he also played a role. His writing had, and has retained, the quiet and courteous firmness of his admirable lectures. Those explosions which have occurred have been rare, and have been such as to illuminate a normally peaceful landscape. At one early point, though, he did step into the fight.

This happened when, in the issue which carried John Wain's poem and Wallace Robson's observations on the insecurity of greatness, he sharply criticised a collection of essays by John Raymond of the *New Statesman*. Frank had no use for John Raymond's errors ('gonfalcon', 'matric', 'esenoplastic'), which may have been the printer's, I imagine, and he refused to listen to pleas about the printer's boy hammering on the door for copy. 'Mr Raymond's knack of concealing his serious interests fails him only when he is speaking of religion and historiography; and his book is worthy to stand beside *Channel Packet* on any shelf where *Channel Packet* stands.' (*Channel Packet* by Raymond Mortimer, a predecessor of John's at the *New Statesman*.) John Raymond was a bookman who liked books, and he was to behave generously over the review when an opportunity for getting his own back arrived. He was indeed a popular journalist, and a partisan of his wrote to the paper in order to praise him, and to add, forgetting all about Gordon Brown, that 'Mr Kermode has never been guilty of amusing *me*.'

One of the amusements of the period I'm talking about, as chronicled in the issues of the paper produced in the first half of 1958, was an advertisement for Lady Diana Cooper's memoir, *The Rainbow Comes and Goes*, which contained tributes from John Raymond and from a man who testified to Lady Diana's 'true sanctity'. That sort of thing too was part of what was going on.

I may have given the impression that Frank Kermode was new to the reading public when he started writing for the paper. That was not the case. He'd already made his name with his fine book *Romantic Image*, a deeply self-expressive contemplation of the Symbolist aesthetic, of its element of supernaturalism, and of 'the great and in some ways noxious historical myth of Symbolism', predicating a 'dissociation of sensibility'. The chapter on T. S. Eliot's idea of a seventeenth-century separation of feeling from thought comparable to the fall of man delivers valuable soundings of the poetry, fiction and literary argument of the modern world. The chapter speaks of the invention, by Eliot and others, of a golden age designed to protect the Symbolist aesthetic by linking it with a past when image and discourse were one and with a crisis when they ceased to be one – a crisis aligned with the passing of Medieval Christianity. The chapter points out that the Symbolist aesthetic forbids paraphrase – a statable content for poetry – while nevertheless allowing it. It draws to a close with the wise words, 'good modern criticism is much more eclectic in method than most theoretical pronouncements suggest', and closes with the suggestion that the dissociative preoccupation with poetry and statement – which has had more to do with keeping them apart, it might seem, than with bringing them together – was best forgotten.

The arguments presented in 1967 in *The Sense of an Ending*, another highly personal book, in which Modernism's projected endings are compared with the aeons and apocalypses of the eschatological systems of the past, are a continuation of the age-of-dissociation arguments presented in *Romantic Image*. The golden age of the unified sensibility reappears in the millennium of certain Modernists – a project which was tainted by adherence to an apocalyptic and authoritarian politics. That taint is not treated in any polemical spirit, but can seldom have been more cogently examined.

Having published *Romantic Image*, Frank went on from book to book along the arterial roads of his principal concerns. But it's also true to say that he went on from piece to piece, that his principal concerns were often to be discovered and addressed in his literary journalism, and that his reviews were to supply the material for several of his books. The contentions and aspirations evident in the literary journalism of his early days helped to form him, and I think it is fair to claim that, for all the defects of tone and temper that can be turned up in the record, the writings compiled by the critics, scholars and popular journalists of the Fifties, acting both at odds and in concert, as one, as a unified sensibility, implaus-ible as that last notion may seem, exhibit an ambition to serve the literature and society of the time.

Times changed for Frank, as times do, and some of his later concerns came to him as a consequence of these changes, though he has also, of course, been an initiator, as in the case of the study of narrative which arose in the

Seventies, and of the interest in the canonical which has arisen since. No other senior British critic has done more to learn from what younger people were doing, and from the climate. It would seem excitable to claim that a different world has ensued, in this quarter, since the events of 1958, but it's easy to understand why the claim can be heard. Lecturers no longer, one feels, write 'Well felt!' in the margins of their students' essays, as was once reported. The old battle between critics and journalists became antediluvian. Puns and footnotes were reconciled, though it can't be thought that all pedantry disappeared, or that peace broke out within the intellectual community. Frank was a superb theorist of literature well before the fact of the new millennial, past-abolishing theory, which has now begun, in this country at least, to abolish itself. He moved on his own terms into the new theory, and then moved out; both moves deserve to be respected. Those who were never in should be ready to accept that both moves showed courage.

Karl Miller

19. BUT LET US LISTEN TO THE MOON

(To Frank Kermode at 80)

The old fantasies are best,
they're easier to rewrite.
How far back this one goes
which locates all mislaid objects
on the moon nobody knows
but Ariosto used it. Well,
someone was on the moon the other day,
it wasn't signposted Moon
but it was certainly full
of lost wits, those who endure
delegates coming and going

85

in lecture rooms with polished desks,
so many souls in chinos,
denim and labelled jackets,
and texts, such dowdy texts –
'Everyone born abroad has lived
at some time or another
in Belsize Park'...
What we're looking for
is our original innocence
or perhaps accountability –
the day we read *The Ancient Mariner*
in the bathroom or had
our first erection flitting
through *Cage Me a Peacock* –
O Moon, we cry aloud,
show us your hermetic pale
where may be heard that fabled cry
The True Voice of Feeling
in The Language That Men Speak,
tell us stories of young men
whose parents never read a book
but whose already paranoid
imaginations opened on to
Realms of Gold. Try the dodgems
at the first of Luna Parks,
navigate the caves of ice
and listen to the Damsel
with the Dulcimer. Moon jokes
are sheer ephemera,
the lustrous replicas
of individual genius
worn down to tropes
of Book Reviews. Astolfo
unsaddles the Hippogriff
and welcomes us; the landscape
reminds us of the river bend
beside the city abbatoirs

but language is in shock –
a voice proclaims
'In these Blue Remaindered Hills
the European Spirit
can scarcely draw a breath
and safe in silver statutes wait
the clichés of the Nation State.'
Then Frank, as someone who has lived
a proper life of scholarship,
consider those strict phases which
bestow on the Confused Ones,
we who litter literature with
our agony of imitation
(not Anxiety of Influence)
a glow as natural as moonlight
reaching here through distant trees
and lighting the sad nocturnals
of a readerly timidity.
We all take up the shining of
The First Great Face
and you, who've set the species'
indirectness in a hinterland
of true accountability,
may you by moonlight never see
a page turned sharply in regret
or something lost not destined to be found.

Peter Porter

20. THE CHAIRMAN

WAS IT WHEN I joined the staff of the Arts
Council of Great Britain in 1966 that I first
met Frank Kermode, who was already a Council member, or had we met earlier during my years as
assistant editor of the *London Magazine*, a monthly lit-

erary journal to which he certainly contributed? I cannot now remember. My earliest recollections are of our sitting around a huge conference table in the Arts Council's lavish headquarters at 105 Piccadilly, either at Council meetings chaired by Lord Goodman, with such distinguished people as Lord Harewood, Sir John Pope-Hennessy, Sir Edward Boyle and Sir William Coldstream, or at meetings of the Council's Literature Advisory Panel chaired by Angus Wilson, with other well-known writers who included Ted Hughes, Peter Porter, Julian Mitchell and William Sansom.

If I had not met Frank before those Arts Council days, I had certainly read him, for he was a frequent contributor of articles and reviews not only to the *London Magazine* but also to the *Spectator*, the *Listener* and *Encounter*. I used to think impudently that, for an academic, his range of interests was impressively wide. He did not specialise in American novels of the twentieth century, or Russian ones of the nineteenth, or *fin de siècle* French literature, or whatever, but was able to write perceptively and authoritatively on a wide variety of subjects. It was he who led me to read William Golding, who opened my eyes to the merits of C. P. Snow, and who reassured me that it was perfectly respectable to be bored by Samuel Beckett.

Those early meetings of the Arts Council's Literature Panel are fascinating to look back upon. When it was set up in 1966, the panel consisted of twenty or more people. Far too many, of course, for sensible discussion; but when I became Literature Director it took me years to reduce the number gradually to twelve. And some members of the panel in those first days were more impressive than others. I remember that Iris Murdoch joined at my urging, but did not stay long for she confessed to me that she found our proceedings unbearably tedious. Leonard Clark, one of the panel members, was a funny little chap, a poet and Inspector of Schools whose main concern seemed to be to promote the poetry of Leonard Clark.

Most of them, however, were well-known literary names, with the exception of Reg Davis-Poynter, a publisher with the engaging air of a wide-boy. Not all were assiduous in their attendance at meetings, and of those who did come regularly one or two hardly opened their mouths except to sip the dreadful Arts Council tea. One of the most helpful members of the panel was the thoughtful and courteous Frank Kermode. Cecil Day Lewis, our amiable chairman, was a sweet man, but his invariable response to all suggestions which he feared might involve him in action of any kind was a tired 'Oh, Lor!'

When Cecil retired at the end of 1967 he was succeeded by Angus Wilson, and Frank then became vice-chairman. At that time, when Arts Council directors had considerably more authority and prestige than they were subsequently to be allowed, it would have been unthinkable for a new Advisory Panel chairman or vice-chairman to have been foisted upon a director without prior consultation. I was always consulted when a change was being proposed, and I remember how delighted I was when, after the elegantly bored Day Lewis and the lovable and effervescent Angus Wilson, Frank's name came up.

I was at that time Assistant Literature Director. When the Director, Eric Walter White, retired in 1971 the post was advertised, but the Council's chairman, Lord Goodman, advised me not to apply, warning me that I was likely to be blackballed by the Arts Minister, who apparently disliked most of my public utterances and thought I was, as Arnold Goodman put it, 'something of a wild man'. Nevertheless, I did apply.

They could hardly have avoided shortlisting me, and in due course I was interviewed by a small committee of Council members which consisted of Lord Goodman, Lady Antonia Fraser and Lawrence Gowing. As

Chairman of the Literature Panel, Frank Kermode should have been one of the committee, but he was abroad. It is thanks to him, however, that I became Literature Director, a job I stayed in for fifteen years, for, when asked by telegram to adjudicate between the merits of the two leading candidates, the poet George Macbeth and myself, Frank had wired his answer back in four words: 'The devil you know.'

Many pictures flash through my mind as I recall those Arts Council years with Frank. In most of them we are sitting around a table, or standing chatting to famous poets at receptions for the Poetry International Festival which Patrick Garland and I directed every summer. But one of the images which comes unbidden to mind is an absurd one. I am in the foyer of the Arts Council one afternoon when Frank enters the building. Normally healthy-looking and upright of posture, on this occasion he walks bent over almost at an angle of ninety degrees. I could not help but be reminded of Groucho Marx; in fact, I was probably crass enough to say so to Frank. He had put his back out somehow, but fortunately the next time we met, some days later, he was his normal self again.

Only recently in a Sunday newspaper column, 'Bibliophile', Frank answered a number of questions. His favourite novelist, he said, is Dostoevsky. Mine too. His favourite play, *Hamlet*. Again, mine. The most difficult book he has ever read? Beckett's *Comment c'est*. Moi aussi! To the question 'Which book should have a sequel?' he answered, 'Musil, *The Man Without Qualities*'. At last, we differ. My answer to that question would have been: 'Whatever Frank Kermode's most recent book is' – at the time of writing, appropriately enough, his wonderful memoir *Not Entitled*.

Charles Osborne

I HAVE KNOWN Frank Kermode for forty years: as his research student, employee, colleague. During that time he has exercised the strongest influence on my professional life – not just my 'career' (such as it is), but more important, my sense of what the profession of teaching, literary scholarship and critical analysis should amount to. He has also become my dearest friend. Many, here and elsewhere, will testify to his loyalty, his warm, laidback wit, his unceasing interest in what one has been up to, his generosity with time and ideas, his practical help. But I want to say something about my first impressions of him, which were much more alienating, if not frightening. It wasn't Frank's fault. He hasn't changed; I have. For one thing, I am no longer a terrified graduate student. But so much else is different too, from the university environment and the way research in the humanities is managed, to the British public sphere itself.

For the newly arrived American England in the late Fifties was a bewildering mixture of formality and social ease, a gracious acceptance of hierarchy and disadvantage: disparities accepted because in the cultural transparency of the metropolis they remained unexamined. You got off the ship in Southampton and travelled up to London in a steam train, on which servants in frogged coats served you tea and cakes at your own little table. From the windows men in collar and tie could be seen digging their allotments. Waterloo Station was awash with thousands of soldiers and sailors, milling around the concourse, lined up along the platforms. Each regiment wore its distinctive uniform of khaki or navy blue, or short jackets and plaid trousers. On their heads were berets, or little pillboxes, or blue peaked caps with red feathers, or the same with the colours reversed. Was there some national emergency? Had war been declared while we Americans were drinking, slumbering and mis-behaving on the Atlantic? No. It was the weekday currency of Empire: men preparing to play their roles in whatever distant part of the world they were being shipped out to.

So incessant was this circulation in and out of the metropolis that it seemed perfectly natural that I should be on my way to England to pursue research in American literature. Granted I was interested in an early colonial poet grounded in the English metaphysicals, but even so the number of English specialists in American literature of any description could then be counted on the fingers of two hands – and most of them were outside the academy. Manchester University was the exception. They even had a department of American studies, and in their young Head of English, Frank Kermode, one of the best Renaissance scholars in the country.

So after the apprenticeship of an MA by dissertation at Cardiff, I applied for a 'Research Studentship in Arts' at Manchester. This obscure award, advertised I think only once a year in a single column inch somewhere in the undergrowth of *The Times* small ads but known mainly by word of mouth, was for £400 – enough then to cover tuition and living expenses for a year. Offering such bounty, it had to be highly competitive. Certainly the rigours of the interview were such as to reinforce that impression.

I left Cardiff at around five in the morning in order to thread my way up the tortuous rail network to get there in time. The muggy morning dawned reluctantly to disclose a sooty landscape of dead-eyed warehouses. Manchester in 1960 was very different from the breezy, well-ordered city so loved by its enormous student population today. The fashion for the 'urban renewal' of disused industrial and commercial sites was still some distance in the future. You got around not by bright new trams, but by buses lumbering along in the November fogs, special lights focused on the kerb to help the drivers find their way. The club scene consisted of an upstairs room heated with a kerosene stove whose only attraction was that it remained open during the afternoon to sell weak beer after the pubs had closed. Manchester was where the journey from your digs to the smoke-blackened Owens Building took you past decayed row houses with broken windows outside of which barefoot kids scuffled in the dirt and coal dust. Not that the Council was indifferent to this squalor. When the Queen came to open the new law courts later that year, the slums across the square were fitted out with stage-set window boxes, and the windows themselves reglazed: not with glass, but with plywood cross-hatched with highlights to look like glass from Her Majesty's safely distant coign of vantage.

Interviews for the studentship were conducted in a similar vein of amiability. After waiting, knees almost touching in the tiny, airless room, the four candidates were taken one by one into a room as cavernous as the antechamber had been restricted, to be confronted by thirty men and one woman seated around an enormous egg-shaped table. I was told to sit at the pointy end of the egg. From down at the round end Professor Kermode was invited to speak to me. He asked something about Yvor Winters, under whom I had studied at Stanford. And, er ..., as *Private Eye* would say, ... that was it. Nothing about my research, or how I thought I might use the studentship, or even whether I'd had a pleasant trip up on the train (I hadn't).

So it was obvious that I hadn't got the money. I was there just to fill out the numbers, make the shortlist look respectable. But wait a minute! As the other candidates emerged, one after the other told the same story. Was none of us to get the award, then? Did no one meet its exacting standards? Or was it just all a big practical joke? We decided to go to lunch. While enjoying the best

93

biriani we had ever eaten, we were joined briefly by one of the professors who had been seated around the table. He put his hands in his pocket, leaned back and said, 'I doubt if you have ... [long pause] ... too much to worry about.' We had all got it. There were four awards available, and the four of us had been selected long before. The 'interview' had just been that term's meeting of the Faculty of Arts. After the serious business they had called us in just to see if we were breathing.

Come the autumn term, we were assigned our supervisors. The good news was that mine was a proper 'Americanist'; the bad that, as he cheerfully admitted, he hadn't the slightest interest in anything American thought, felt or written before 1850. What could I do about this shattering revelation, which made nonsense of my pilgrimage to Manchester, not to mention my wonderful (if mysteriously acquired) studentship? Miserable as I was, I didn't feel I could go whingeing to the Head of Department: some remnant of the code of the Old West prevented that, together with my blank ignorance about how such things were done in England.

But as it happened, out of general curiosity about the place to which I was headed, I had read what I think were the only two things that Frank had published by then: his Arden edition of *The Tempest* and the British Council pamphlet on John Donne. The latter was and remains the best succinct survey of the poet's intellectual and theological interests, sensibility and rhetorical procedures. The edition was, if anything, even more remarkable. Accomplished in under a year when he was still in his mid-thirties, Kermode's *Tempest* provided not only the exacting textual editing and annotation that would occupy other Arden editors for a lifetime – or defeat them altogether before they died of old age – but also a set of appendices extracted from contemporary documents, and an introduction of nearly a hundred pages setting the play so comprehensively in its historical, intellectual and discursive context that even today every serious student of the British early-modern period has to use the book: intellectual historians and post-colonial theorists, as well as students of literature.

Although not very good at smooth career decisions, much less lateral thinking, even I could work out that I might be better off studying with a Renaissance scholar of Kermode's ability and attainments. As it happens, the chance to put the question informally arose quite quickly. After a lecture he gave at the John Rylands Library, Frank offered me a lift home. And it was there, crouching forward in the back seat of his Austin 1100, that I blurted out my plea to be taken on as his research student. It was clear that his interests were really much closer to mine, I explained. Could some arrangement be worked out?

Despite my obvious eagerness – or perhaps because of it – the answer wasn't definitive. Frank said that of course I could come and see him from time to time, perhaps even sit in on his third-year honours seminar on the English metaphysicals. And that was how it worked. No formal transfer of supervisors was effected, but Frank became my de facto academic adviser from then on. I realised later that we had gone through a peculiarly English manoeuvre, one which did the business without hurting feelings. As proof of its success, my ex-supervisor and I remained friends (he must have been mightily relieved to have got shot of me), and my respect, admiration and love for Frank have lasted to this day. And he was, it need hardly be said, a superb guide to the complexities, not only of the research, but of getting a job after it.

At first it wasn't easy, though. The trouble with Frank was that he was so unlike the high and mighty academic figures I had come to know, whether in art or life. He certainly dressed differently from American professors. Granted, he smoked a pipe, but he sported no tweed jacket with leather patches on the elbows; rather a neat suit and maroon fabric waistcoat, accented by sharply horn-rimmed glasses. Though his dress sense has mellowed over the years – indeed, more in the direction of classic academic attire – he looked then more like a provincial bank manager. Nor was he James Robertson Justice, hectoring, terrorising and ultimately charming his first-year medical students in *Doctor in the House*. None of that silky, gossipy culture rumoured to infest Oxbridge, either. Although he must have had his ambitions, they didn't show. He was not the great man, more often at conferences than in the university – or, as with the American equivalent, present only at the far end of a big lecture theatre, never face to face, one to one. For every student, from first-year to postgraduate, Frank was available, in person, when and for as long as they needed him. Most unexpected of all, at least then, he wrote not only papers, but for the papers. Within the same week he would finish a learned essay on the iconographical context of Chapman's *Ovids Banquet of Sence*, while reviewing contemporary fiction and criticism for the *New Statesman*.

For all that, though, it was months before I could feel at ease with him, especially in the individual supervisions. His combination of immense learning and (as it seemed to me then) very English coolness produced an authority, however unintended on his part, that was just too powerful for a personal relationship with a graduate student. At least it had the effect of making me do things. Part of my work entailed reading in the texts of biblical exegesis. I remember him saying once, 'You might have a look at the *Patrologia Latina*.' The what? Would that, as it were, be in Latin? Yes, it was. Moreover, its volumes filled two whole shelves in the Manchester University Library. Where – how – was I going to start on that? Then when I was done, maybe I could move on to the *Patrologia Graeca*. I should, of course, have to learn

Greek. So I did – or at least enough to make it through some of the simpler commentaries.

Spoon-feeding it was not. But it wasn't impossible. As I found out soon enough, there was a trick to it. Biblical commentaries are keyed to texts, after all, and I had only a finite number of texts to check out. And the Latin and Greek involved in the checking, read only for basic content, are not really very complex – much beneath the rhetorical and lexical level required of, say, an A-level classics student. But after a near-career of supervising PhDs of my own, not to mention founding and running a graduate research centre in the humanities, I do sometimes wonder how such guidance, how such an environment for living and working, would sit with today's graduate students, or the British Academy, or the Higher Education Funding Councils, come to that. And I wonder sometimes whether my closeness to Frank now doesn't have at least something to do with my having been scared shitless of him when I was *in statu pupillari*.

Stephen Fender

22. SEIGNEUR FRANK

Natives of poverty, children of malheur,
The gaiety of language is our seigneur.

Wallace Stevens, 'Esthetique du Mal'

WONDERING WHAT I might want to say about Frank Kermode on this occasion, I recall a little episode some thirty years ago when I was visiting him in London. It's lodged in my mind because of a remark of his, a mere interpolation, that nonetheless made me aware of something vitally important about him. He had given me a recording of Mozart's Sinfonia

Concertante for violin, viola and orchestra, the exquisite K364, and while we were listening to it with other guests of his that evening, two of them started a conversation. Their talk was quiet but rather persistent, about some matter having nothing to do with the music. It was a badly timed disruption, coming as it did during the beautifully quiet Andante movement, with its long flow of sustained melody. It was then that I heard him intervene, very gently, as if speaking to himself, and it had the immediate effect of restoring quiet, leaving us to the music: 'imagine being able to write like that,' he said, 'and at twenty-three!'

The remark carried a hint of amazement, especially because he would have been aware, as some of us apparently weren't, that the evidence of Mozart's genius didn't emerge suddenly with this piece, in 1779; there is evidence of it still earlier, in compositions written even before he turned twenty. What we hear in later Mozart are ever more subtle elaborations of the miraculous resources available to him late in his teens. I took Frank's little intervention as addressed more to the music itself than to any of his guests, an expression of wonder at the mystery of creative genius as it could be felt by an intent listening to such a piece, or, as he has been showing all his life, by an intent listening to a poem.

In this age of Theory, the word genius is scarcely to be heard at all. It has more or less disappeared, thanks to the processes of what is called demystification brought to the appreciation of literature. The term 'literature' has itself been appropriated to describe any kind of writing, including advertising copy. Some New Historicists in particular have managed to put the plays of Shakespeare in a relation of rough equality with historical documents with which the plays allegedly share a vocabulary. Even before the 'French invasion', as Kermode calls it in *Not Entitled*, and hoping simply to keep his graduate students at University College informed about new developments, he had begun in the late Sixties and early Seventies to hold small, informal gatherings, gradually developing them into the first seminars in England on French theorists like Lévi-Strauss, Barthes, who attended one meeting of the seminar, and Lacan. He can therefore speak with more authority and balance on the ultimate consequences for the study of literature than can any of his contemporaries in England or the United States, and he receives, accordingly, more respectful attention from proponents of theory, though little agreement, when he laments the degree to which theory has largely displaced the study of literature in English and American universities, making the capacity to recognise and appreciate the workings of poetic language pretty close to extinct in the practice of criticism.

Kermode is emphatic about the disastrous results of this development, most notably in *An Appetite for Poetry* (1989) and in his preface, also in 1989, to a new edition of his *Wallace Stevens*, originally published in 1960. His *Stevens* remains in my estimation still the most penetrating study of that poet and one that will continue to persuade its readers that, in Stevens's own words, 'the words of the world are the life of the world'. As he comes to the end of his preface to *Stevens*, he is more passionate even than in *An Appetite for Poetry* for the losses entailed in our loss of poetry, our understanding, that is, of what poetry can offer so long as the capacity for reading it doesn't altogether atrophy:

The amazing history of modern academic literary criticism seems to show that we are now in the state of finding almost anything more agreeable, or at any rate less difficult, than poetry; gossip about the private lives of poets is best of all, but in the absence of gossip – and in Stevens there isn't a lot to hook on to – then even philosophy comes more easily than poetry. Critics who systematise Stevens, work out what, under all his vatic obscurities, his tranced and sometimes impassioned memesis of thinking, he was really getting at, have at times come quite close to making him a bore. The matter is of concern not only to the people who actually do the damage, and who presumably at some point supposed that they loved and admired the poetry. We are all losers, for the wrong sort of attention is what in the long or short run diminishes a poet for everybody; and a single poet is not all we risk losing ... Our loss if Stevens were to be driven into some enclosure where only the PhDs and their instructors were deemed capable of dealing with his thought, would be greater still, in that in some sense – admittedly hard to define – the scope of Stevens's mind, as we apprehend it in the wonderful mass of poetry he wrote in his sixties and seventies, is roughly coextensive with that of the modern mind and sensibility; the range of his reflections, after the death of God, still covers most of what we think of as possible in our condition, a condition which Stevens repeatedly calls 'poverty' ... his fundamental richness lay in his sense of poverty and of poetry as its quite natural mitigation, merely his version of what everybody needs to live in the world:

> a single shawl
> Wrapped tightly round us, since we are poor, a warmth,
> A light, a power, the miraculous influence.

When a people lose an 'appetite for poetry' – poetry, that is, with such exploratory energies and disruptive-creative densities as can be found in the language of Stevens – then they are at the same time on the way to losing a reverence for language as an indispensable cultural inheritance and, still more, as an instrument for cultural change and renewal. We are deprived of a precious exemplification of how any of us might use the language of everyday life with some of the spirited inventiveness found in the best poetry, to use it in order to confront and transform, if only for the duration of utterance, some of the constituted realities around us and the inevitability of death.

An 'appetite for poetry' is, to an extent, an acquired taste. And yet as Stevens makes clear in his essays, it is something that belongs in some degree, and even if they don't know it does, to everyone, whether they can read poetry or not. Ordinary speech is often full of what Stevens means by the 'gaiety of language'. 'Those of us,' he writes in 'The Noble Rider and the Sound of Words', 'who may have been thinking of the path of poetry, those of us who understand that words are thoughts and not only our own thoughts but the thoughts of men and women ignorant of what it is they are thinking, must be conscious of this: that poetry is words; and that words are, above everything else, sounds.'

These sounds, literally the sounds of life that are to be heard in a poem, remain always alive within it, generating new possibilities of meaning long after the death of the poet. They are likely to go undetected, however, when left to the kind of tutelage now offered in the classroom, and when nearly any of us may in any event lose some capacity to hear the sounds that are in poetry when the language of TV and of political rallying have so effectively blocked out hearing. But just as the life in the words of a poem can survive the death of the poet who wrote it, it can, in its neglected state, survive a culture that lives in ignorance of it. The subject of Stevens, most serenely and most powerfully evident in the late poems written in the years immediately before his death, is, as Kermode writes, simply this: 'living without God and finding it good, because of the survival of the power that once made him suffice'.

The poems of the last years are, according to the preface to the 1989 edition of *Stevens*, 'his finest work – for me the greatest poems in English about death and old age, and possibly about anything'. Kermode is a notably meticulous writer, and, I suspect, the most widely read of critic-scholars, someone who can convincingly allude in so sweeping a way to 'poems in English'. No less so when using a phrase like 'anything else'. The phrase isn't meant at all casually: it has reference to the extraordinary degree to which the syntax of these poems can manage continuously to take us beyond considerations of anything that seems to be specifically alluded or referred to in the poem's language.

In 'The River of Rivers in Connecticut', for instance, the river is indeed said to be in Connecticut, flowing past two specifically named towns in a state where Stevens lived most of his life and where he will, in a few years, die. This is home territory for him. And yet the river is referred to not simply as 'local' but as a 'local abstraction'. It is an 'unnamed flowing', its water *is* 'a gayety', he says, reminding us that for him, so too, famously, is the play of language. The language of this river is, it would seem, necessarily vaguer about what it might refer to than is the often designedly vague language of Stevens's own poems, especially the late ones. It is a 'third commonness' along with 'light and air', bringing to mind the epigraph for his earlier 'Evening without Angels': 'The great interests of man; air and light, the joy of having a body, the voluptuousness of looking.' The river isn't said to be *like* 'a curriculum, a vigor'. It *is* these things, just as it *is* 'a gayety'. We are told twice over in a mere eighteen lines, and as if any name would prove inadequate, to 'call it once more', simply, 'a river', and, in the last two lines, enjoined to '... call it again and again, / The river that flows nowhere, like the sea.' The poem disclaims any hints of specific referentiality: we are left with abstractions beyond which poetry and the criticism of it cannot go: words like Life or the life force. More important still, the creativity of the poet, his powers of figuration, seem willingly to let themselves be absorbed into the powerful movement of this river. In the sound and movement of the poem, Stevens as a presence seems no more distinct than water is in water:

> There is a great river this side of Stygia,
> Before one comes to the first black cataracts
> And trees that lack the intelligence of trees.

In that river, far this side of Stygia,
The mere flowing of the water is a gayety,
Flashing and flashing in the sun. On its banks,

No shadow walks. The river is fateful,
Like the last one. But there is no ferryman.
He could not bend against its propelling force.

It is not to be seen beneath the appearances
That tell of it. The steeple at Farmington
Stands glistening and Haddam shines and sways.

It is a third commonness with light and air,
A curriculum, a vigor, a local abstraction ...
Call it, once more, a river, an unnamed flowing.

Space-filled, reflecting the seasons, the folk-lore
Of each of the senses; call it, again and again,
The river that flows nowhere, like the sea.

Though Kermode has not, so far as I can discover, ever written about this poem and though he does not, in conversations with me at least, ever undertake to discuss it, he has on several recent occasions mentioned it with a fascinated reverence. It seems appropriate that Kermode, this great master of criticism and of what it can do, should love a poem he doesn't discuss and that fills him with a pleasure indistinguishable from the pleasure of being alive.

Richard Poirier

4

PARTICULARITIES

With Tony Tanner

Numbers themselves that ceased to sing
And in vers libre lay languishing
    Today forsake the shades
    In which good faith evades

The glare of spotlights, and the glitz
Celebratory praise emits
    When Fine Works fall in shame
    To cheap, post-modern Fame,

Unsent fan-mail, far-too-short
Unbusied thanks, curtailed report,
    Unexpressed feelings, all
    Out of the woodwork crawl

And hasten straightly to be penned
In lines by a retiring friend
    Joining in singsong those
    More learned ones in prose

To hail the rarest kind of name
That rhymes so faithfully with fame:
    John (ineffable)
    Frank (free, open, full)

(The first, mine too, admittedly,
By these these he would become for me
    – My father's was the other –
    A sort of older brother)

Knowledge of whom began (and love
Thereafter came to follow) – of
    Which I now recall
    Started in the fall

Knowledge of whom I now remember
First began early in September
    Of 1952
    (Of this, a word or two:)

Helping a college friend unpack
The books that he had had shipped back
    From Cambridge, where he'd spent
    The last two years – anent

A small pale green anthology
Of *English Pastoral Poetry*
    Edited by Frank
    Kermode: 'Who's that?' – I thank

My friend for his reply –
'O, he's the smartest younger guy
    Around' – a view I found
    To be completely sound.

But then in 1962
A somewhat favourable review
    I read by him of my
    The Untuning of the Sky

Saying it was 'too long, and too
Expensive' may have been quite true.
    (Yet young, I'd not the gift
    Of seldom feeling miffed.)

But then we came to meet not long
Thereafter – if I'm now not wrong –
    He was living quite near
    At Wesleyan, for a year,

Thereupon always taking note
And pleasure of everything he wrote

Admiring what it took
To map such worlds of book;

Then starting with *The Sense of an
Ending* our dear friend's work began
       To see both Book and World
       In one conclusion curled

Guiding us to comprehend
What lies beyond the River's bend
       Whether the flow of Time
       Or that of prose or rhyme

Before poor *closure* had become
Discursively so very dumb
       For journalistic rabble
       A piece of psychobabble

The Genesis of Secrecy
Once again astonished me:
       The enigmatic and
       Elliptical withstand

In it the best combined attacks
Of the most commonsense-less hacks
       (*Die Narren*, they must be,
       Of *narratologie*).

Sharing generously with me
An appetite for poetry
       His highest art of telling
       Forms of attention, spelling

Out the lines by which it occurred
That the romantic images got blurred,
       As in a Pauline mirror:
       The uses of our error.

Lest long, uncritical acclaim
Like mine unwittingly defame
    (When timid brevity
    Decamps, dull levity

Comes creeping in); so, in good cheer,
Let the few books I've mentioned here
    Metonymic, stand
    For the whole proud and grand

List of the volumes that have shone
Unshaking light upon our own
    Reflections that returned
    Something of what we'd learned.

Standing between the all too slow
Or trivially rushing flow
    Of Tedium or Whimsy
    Firm among the flimsy

Strings of Potemkin villages
That criticism often is
    His Works were built so well
    We all therein yet dwell.

Through academic thin and thick
Whose last two decades leave one sick
    He wisely kept his head
    And taught us all instead

– Flying above such noisome strife –
The lively art of artful life
    Which firmly to maintain
    Is thereby more to gain.

John Hollander

24. SO BLOODY CLEAR

AFTER SYNGE had entered the Abbey Theatre, he would, it is said, sit quietly until the celebrated tenor, John McCormack appeared; then Synge would bellow, 'There he is again! Always so bloody clear!' Frank, now no longer not entitled, has always written with ease and force – and with scintillant clarity about complex matters, especially about the fugitive connections between art and life. The art of *Samson Agonistes* and the life of Milton in old age, the art of *The Tempest* and Shakespeare's reading, the art of Eliot and his mother's verse ('reminiscent' of Donne on Elizabeth Drury): Always so bloody clear!

I was fortunate in my teachers, though the contrast between my undergraduate and graduate studies aroused in me unfortunate feelings about the profession I saw myself entering. At Amherst College my teachers devoted themselves to 'slow reading', their version of what came to be known as the New Criticism. My classmates and I learned the language of irony and paradox but could not always be sure that Dryden preceded Pope... At Stanford – then a provincial university with, nevertheless, redoubtable scholars in Renaissance literature – my teachers believed, some without question, in the efficacy of the kind of historical scholarship that even then we were beginning to dismiss as 'positivistic'. I now knew, in this diachronic environment, that Dryden wrote before Pope, and I felt that someday I might be able to practise what I was already referring to as the New Philology; but I could discover no way to relate the critical study of literature to the exercise of historical scholarship. It was all PMLA to me.

I shall always be grateful to my teachers at Amherst and Stanford; they taught me whatever it is that I think I know, but it remained, until halfway through graduate school, a tale of two institutions, of two ways of knowing, that seemed unalterably opposed. Although J. V. Cunningham, with irony always verging on sarcasm, had convinced me that criticism divorced from historical scholarship was open, and rightly open, to ridicule, I had to wait for Kermode to suggest, through his exemplary practice, ways in which I might reconcile Amherst to Stanford, New Criticism to intellectual and cultural history. No need to overdramatise the moment. I was also reading the likes of M. H. Abrams, Erich Auerbach, Kenneth Burke, E. R. Curtius, Ernst Kantorowicz, Leo Spitzer. Nevertheless, it was the shock of recognition, my encounter with *Romantic Image* in 1957, that showed me the way, that lent me the confidence to read 'The Horatian Ode' neither as Cleanth Brooks wanted me to read it nor as Douglas Bush didn't want me to read it but rather as Marvell (I liked this way of thinking about it) might have wanted me to read it. Intentional Fallacy! With the Heresy of Paraphrase quivering on the horizon! To do this sort of thing in my own, and limited, way, I would have to accustom myself to be on the lookout, as was Kermode (and Abrams), for the underlying assumptions that explained the otherwise inexplicable, and I had to learn to cheat, as nearly as possible in the manner of Kermode.

What caught, then fixed, my attention was the movement of his mind as, to paraphrase Eliot on Marvell, Frank made his points with utmost clarity while yet showing his awareness of other kinds of experience that are possible. First the assumptions shaping the 'Romantic Image', then the way these assumptions dictate present-day thinking about literature: 'What still prevails is the Symbolist conception of the work of art as aesthetic monad, as the product of a mode of cognition superior to, and different from, that of the sciences. Any alternative is likely to be treated as heretical ...' Finally the need, in these circumstances, to do some cheating. As a result of this 'orthodoxy' about works of art the 'practical business of criticism becomes enormously strenuous' (phrasing that anticipates the day when professors at Yale look into the abyss or when those at Duke clash on just about any darkling plain) and provokes a 'good deal of cheating'. The critic must not appeal to 'authorial intention', must not appear 'to believe in paraphrase' or, indeed in 'any form of historical approach'; and yet, of course, the better critic will have (covert) recourse to these and other 'forbidden techniques'. It almost goes without saying that as a graduate student plunged deep in historical research I found it irresistible, this invitation on the part of a writer flashing impeccable scholarly credentials to reach for the tree of forbidden techniques.

The reviewing and the higher journalism, the sense of endings in poetry and intellectual history, the acumen in disclosing the genesis of secrecy, the insights into Hawthorne and figuralism – all these exhibit Sir Frank's range and his talent for detailed analysis of, say, the weight and heft of a poetic line, all these held together by the persisting concern with interpretation (in its various forms) and the steady reliance on history (in its various forms), all these in the service of what Eliot took to be the first task of criticism, the elucidation of works of art. Although *Romantic Image* holds its special place in my intellectual development (the plucking of those 'forbidden techniques'), the arrival of each new essay, review, lecture, edition, address and book by the cosmopolitan Manxman leads me to think: 'There he is again! Always so bloody clear!'

Edward Tayler

25. THE TOMB OF PETRARCH'S LAURA

ONE OF SIR WALTER RALEIGH'S commendatory sonnets to his friend Edmund Spenser, 'A Vision upon this conceipt of the *Faery Queene*', begins

> Me thought I saw the graue where *Laura* lay,
> Within that Temple, where the vestall flame
> Was wont to burne, and passing by that way,
> To see the buried dust of liuing fame,
> Whose tombe faire loue, and fairer vertue kept,
> All suddenly I saw the Faery Queene ...

The soul of Petrarch, Raleigh goes on, weeps to find someone and something so much more beautiful and memorable than his own beloved and his own celebration of her in his Canzoniere as to make that memorial of her pass into oblivion.

By Raleigh's time, Petrarch's Laura had become the model for and the surpasser of countless equivalent real or ideal beloveds among the English sonneteers, let alone the Italian poets who had first taken up the Petrarchan mode and the French who had followed them in it. The dead Laura, on the other hand, had had particular attention only from Petrarch himself in the 103 components of the *Sonetti in morte di Madonna Laura*. Less from the imitators, who were celebrating a lady who was living, if unattainable.

Among the *Sonetti in morte*, nevertheless, 'Standomi un giorno solo alla finestra' had always been famous as the 'Canzone delle visioni'. It had been translated by – among others – Clément Marot, Jan van der Noot and Spenser himself. In it, Laura's end is pictured in six different metaphorical forms: *una fera con fronte umana* hunted down by hounds and killed 'under a rock', a ship wrecked by a sudden storm, a bay-tree struck by lightning, a nymph-frequented grove swallowed up in earth, a phoenix killing itself with its beak and Laura-Eurydice stung to death by a serpent at her heel. The 'Canzone delle visioni' was illustrated more often than any other poem in Canzoniere manuscripts, it is the only one to have appeared before 1756 in engraving or woodcut, and it was also pictured, in the sixteenth century, on the walls of Petrarch's house in Arquà.

For van der Noot's French *Theatre* and his Dutch *Toneel* of 1568, Marcus Gheeraerts the Elder made etchings, which were copied in reverse in woodcut for the *Theatre for Worldlings* of 1569. Only in the first vision, however, do etchings or woodcut give an indication of where Laura's remains might lie: the rock under which the hind, in whose form she is shown, is about to be killed. In one rendering of this vision only does there appear an elaborate tomb, and that is the superb drawing by Rosso Fiorentino, of the 1530s, now in Christ Church, Oxford.

Raleigh could hardly have known this drawing and, though he might well have been familiar with the etchings or the woodcut – or, just possibly, with one or other of two emblematic manuscripts of the 'Canzone delle visioni', made on the basis of Marot's translation – he is surely not referring to them in his sonnet, which makes clear that Laura's grave is in a convent. By his time, indeed, an aspect of the cult of Laura had long been an interest in the places where she lived and died. The exact spot of Laura's interment was widely believed to be – and widely visited, though not by Raleigh – in the Franciscan convent in Avignon.

Petrarch himself is responsible for this belief. From his day to this, doubts have been maintained as to whether Laura ever had the real existence which he maintained she did. Not only did he tell how he had ordered her portrait from Simone Martini but, on a flyleaf of the manuscript of Virgil, now in the Biblioteca Ambrosiana at

Milan, executed to his order and later given a superb frontispiece, again to his order, by Simone Martini, he wrote what is known as the 'Nota di Laura'. This records his first sight of the beloved, in Avignon, at early mass in the church of St Clare on 6 April 1327, her death exactly twenty-one years later, and her interment, at Vesper-time on the same day, in the the same Franciscan church there.

The earliest biographies of Petrarch make no mention of Laura, but the fifteenth- and sixteenth-century growth of the Petrarchan fashion brought with it a demand for biographical detail, as well as for what the great Pierre de Nolhac characterised as 'ce besoin de satisfaire l'imagination par les yeux, qui a causé tant de déconvenues à la recherche iconographique'. In the 1480s, her portrait was already being identified in frescoes at Avignon, and her original being sought for in the vicinity, by Italian travellers. The most influential Petrarchan commentator, Alessandro Velutello, spent much time there before identifying her as one Laure de Chiabaud; others had decided on Laure de Noves, who married Hugues de Sade in 1325. In his discourse on Laura's origins, appearing in countless editions of the *Rime* from 1525 onwards, Velutello makes no mention of her tomb apart from the bald statement, quoting the 'Nota di Laura', of the fact and the place of her interment. A few years after Velutello, Mgr Bontempo, vicar of the Bishop of Avignon, Cardinal Ippolito de' Medici, perhaps – or it may have been Girolamo Mannelli di Rocca Contrada, a Florentine gentleman, later Bishop of Nocera – supplemented French rage for all things and all persons Petrarchan. In 1533, it seems, they set the poet Maurice Scève to search for Laura's tomb. Or was François I the instigator? It is not easy to tell, for our sole witness to Scève's enterprise is the grossly flattering account published by Jean de Tournes in *Il Petrarcha*, which he issued at Lyons in 1545 and which was many times reprinted. Scève was certainly in Avignon by that time, but that is about the only verifiable feature of de Tournes's narrative. According to him, at any rate, Scève was immediately successful. In the Chapel of the Holy Cross, the de Sade chapel, first on the right in the church of the Franciscan convent in Avignon, was found 'une grande pierre sans aucune lettre ni autre signe inscrit, sauf deux écus d'armes effacés par le temps'. The friars assured Scève that this was indeed Laura's tomb and Bontempo ordered it to be opened. Within was, along with a quantity of earth, a jawbone, a leaden box bound with copper wire, a sheet of parchment folded and sealed with green wax, a bronze medal, with a blank reverse and on the obverse the figure of a lady, very slim, drawing her robe about her breast, with the letters M L M I above her, which were interpreted to signify MADONNA LAURA MORTE IACE. Scève contrived to read what was on the parchment: an Italian sonnet to Laura. Petrarch's, of course – but it could not be found among his genuine works and in any case was so feeble that immediate Italian denunciation of it as a fake, led by Pietro Bembo, was certainly justified. Scève himself also wrote an epigram to commemorate the occasion.

On 8 September (the Virgin's birthday) 1533 François I, de Tournes goes on, hearing the news on his way to Marseilles to meet Pope Clement VII, made a detour to Avignon and used his royal privilege to have the tomb reopened. His emotions overflowed into a verse epitaph:

> En petit lieu compris vous pouvez veoir
> Ce qui comprent beaucoup par renommée;
> Plume, labeur, la langue et le debvoir
> Furent vaincus de l'amant par l'aymée.
> O gentille ame, estant tant estimée,
> Qui la pourra louer, qu'en se taisant?
> Car la parolle est tousjours reprimée
> Quand le subget surmonte le disant.

No other record of François's visit survives; nor is there any evidence save local tradition that he ordered a splendid tomb to be prepared, but failed to provide the money. It is just possible that Rosso's drawing is somehow related to such a project.

It was left to one Gabriele Symeoni in 1557, according to himself, to restore the tomb, adding a suitable inscription:

D. O. M. S.
ET MEMORIAE AETERNAE,
D. LAURAE, CVM PVDICI-
TIA TVM FORMA FOE-
MINAE INCOMPARABILIS,
QVAE ITA VIXIT, VT
EIVS MEMORIA NVLLO
SAECVLO EXTINGVI
POSSIT.
RESTITVIT VETE-
RVM MONVMENTO-
RVM PEREGRINVS
INDAGATOR
Gabriel Symeonus Flor. IIII.
Idus Aprilis
M. D. LVII.

Symeoni's *Epitaffi*, also published by de Tournes, in 1558, repeats the account of the discovery, gives François's epitaph and has woodcuts of the medal, lettered M L A L, and of his own new epitaph.

The legend of François I, his visit and his epitaph lived long. It was known to André Thevet in 1571, to Nicolas Audebert in 1583 and to Henry Peacham in 1622, who has François proclaiming:

Shame it was that he who sung his Mistresse praise seauen yeares before her death, and twelue yeares [after] should want an Epitaphe.

The tomb figures in Latin verses by one Louis Aleaulme at the end of the sixteenth century, and in the account of the entry of Henri IV's new Queen, Marie de Médicis, into Avignon in 1601. Images of both Petrarch and Laura said to have been copied from it were circulating in the seventeenth century.

Much later, romantic sensibility took up the legend. Early nineteenth-century French history painting showed François in the act of writing his epitaph on, or merely contemplating with his mistress, an elaborate tomb, which had been transferred to Petrarch's Vaucluse and the banks of the Sorgue. A singular account, of 1819, places Laura's tomb in the chapel of St Nicolas, at Lagnes, in Vaucluse.

By that time, Laura's grave and Petrarch's Vaucluse had long been *Sehenswürdigkeiten*. John Evelyn, among others, in October 1644: '... most admired ... the Tomb of Madonna Laura ...' Was this, one wonders, still distinguished somehow by the new epitaph Symeoni claims to have placed to mark it? Perhaps so, because in 1789, though Arthur Young found 'nothing but a stone in the pavement, with a figure engraven on it partly effaced, surrounded by an inscription in Gothic letters', he also found 'another in the wall adjoining'. Or perhaps not, because the second inscription was adorned 'with the armorial of the family of Sade'. That family had long claimed Laura for one of them, and may well have taken matters into its own hands.

The agent in this was perhaps a seventeenth-century scion. In the 1630s the family was claiming possession of the true likeness of Laura. Giacomo Filippo Tomasini published an engraving of it in 1650, versions in oils exist, and there are other engravings in the influential *Mémoires de la vie de Pétrarque* (1764), by the abbé J.-F.-X. de Sade. He may even be responsible for the inscription seen by Young. Box, medal and parchment are said to have remained long with the Franciscans, but in 1756 the enquiring abbé was told by their Provincial that they had been sold – *sans doute*, by some *sous-sacristan* – to a milord on his Grand Tour.

Coming at last to the remark that Raleigh must have

known some of this fantasy reminds me of Frank's inscription in my treasured copy of his Arden *Tempest* (1954), still the best, with its superb introduction:

... the exposition and explanation of authors, which resteth in annotations and commentaries; wherein it is over usual to blanch the obscure places, and discourse upon the plain ...

It was a proud moment when I was allowed to discourse on 'Nobody' in that edition. And it is to Frank and to the late Donald Gordon, senior colleagues at Reading long ago, that I owe my entry to the Warburg Institute and so the forty-six happy years I have spent there. To them, too, I owe most of what understanding I have of Renaissance poetry – much of it acquired through conversations with Frank on the banks of the Thames, some in the unlikely environment of the Thames Conservancy slip.

J. B. Trapp

26. FORAYS AND INTERVENTIONS

I HAVE HAD ONLY two awkward occasions with Sir Frank in many years, but I had better confess to them.

The first was a talk I gave to his graduate seminar at Manchester, where I made the mistake of discussing William Carlos Williams. My head was full of Yeats and Eliot at the time, but I was trying to extend my range of tones and determined to think of Williams as a major poet. Besides, I was in correspondence with him and disposed to like whatever he wrote. But I should have expected that Frank would find Williams's work small American beer, Miller Lite. If your mind is engrossed, as Frank's is and was, with the Bible, Dante, Shakespeare, Donne, Milton, Yeats, Eliot, Valéry, Lawrence, Conrad and Stevens, you would hardly be ready to take

Williams's rapid transit systems seriously. Years later, Hugh Kenner offered to explain why English critics – I'm sure he had Frank in mind – have no ear for Williams's music. Modern English poetry, Kenner maintained, is predicated on Shakespeare and the Elizabethan theatre: hence its reliance on the echoes and recesses of 'words in the dark'. American culture has never had a theatre: instead it has had Franklin and sundry pamphleteers, their concerns fulfilled by *sermo humilis*, a sharp eye, and a plain sense of things. English critics can't listen to Williams or Marianne Moore because they can't hear Shakespeare in their poems. At Manchester I hadn't read Kenner's essay, so I was not equipped to deal with any of this.

The second occasion was a quiet rebuke. I reviewed Stevens's *Letters* in the *New York Review of Books*. Frank told me he didn't like the review; I hadn't got past the quaintness of the letters or Stevens's fussing with the problem of securing the finest brands of tea from Ceylon. There were far more substantial issues than such exotica. Looking at the review again, I thought Frank's rebuke entirely just.

So now: thanks for nearly everything. There is so much to admire: the latitude of Frank's contexts, the learning so urbanely carried, the quality of the writing, the many forms of his attentiveness. His method? He has no method, except the one that Eliot recommended, that of being very intelligent. Indeed, Frank has been severe on those critics – Northrop Frye, as a notable case in point – who have devised a method and kept it in constant employment. He made an exception in favour of Barthes, but mainly because he thought that the method, used on Balzac's *Sarrasine*, yielded extraordinary perceptions. But generally Frank dislikes the machinery of a method and thinks it is likely to get in the way of the works it addresses. 'Method in criticism,' he says, 'is good in so far as it approximates, like the horn on an absey, to transparency.' As for Theory: Frank paid his dues to it for some years when Structuralism was in force, and when Deconstruction was a new critique of Structuralism worth attending to in the writings of Derrida and de Man. He has helped us to understand the theory of fiction, not only in Stevens and Vaihinger but in the practices of novelists. He is willing to be theoretical when the theory helps us to read a poem or a novel. But in recent years he has decided that Theory, now that it has become an institution, is a nuisance: it prevents us from reading works of literature, the only thing that matters. He is still much concerned with theories – theories of meaning, significance, intentionality and value – but not with Theory as an independent form of ratiocination.

In academic scholarship and criticism, Frank admires two kinds of achievement. The first is scholarship that makes available new material, new incitements to thinking: Curtius on the Latin Middle Ages, Auerbach on modes of representation and the development of a literary language – Dante's Italian to begin with, Frances Yates's work on Bruno, the art of memory and the occult, Gombrich on perception, Beryl Smalley on the Bible in the Middle Ages. The second achievement Frank admires is that of powerful, eccentric sensibilities acting on their own authority: Eliot on Dante, Empson on Gray's 'Elegy', Allen Tate on his own 'Ode to the Confederate Dead', Blackmur on the literature of the *anni mirabiles* 1921–1925, Walter Benjamin on Leskov, Baudelaire, Proust and Kafka, Edmund Wilson on the Symbolism he understood and disliked.

How to describe Frank's own criticism? It is not as unperturbed or as imperial as it seems, though he is responsive, not only in *The Classic*, to the values that Eliot spoke up for in his essays on Virgil, Dante and Kipling. Frank's books have what Stevens called 'a peculiarity'. 'A poem,' Stevens said, 'must have a peculiarity, as if it were the momentarily complete idiom of that which prompts it.' 'Momentarily' allows for the equivocal character of the peculiarity. I never feel, reading Frank's essays and books, that the argument is steadily exemplifying a case already made or annotating an official view of things. Everything that Frye wrote after *Anatomy of Criticism* is a set of footnotes to that summa, further illustrations of the method and the poetic myth it served. Frank hasn't written a summa, he likes to keep his mind open to the possibility of being affronted or, in some unpredictable way, delighted. His prejudices keep his peculiarity alive. One such prejudice is a preference for continuity rather than schism. He likes to be able to show that a particular book, apparently wild or otherwise formless, has some saving trace or grace of continuity with the values it appears to scorn. In an early essay on Beckett's *Molloy, Malone Dies* and *The Unnamable*, he said:

One may as well allow these books to succeed in their determined attempt to defeat comment. They are almost entirely unsuccessful; we ought to be frank about this, because literary people are usually too willing to take the will for the deed.

Unsuccessful as what? Frank didn't say. He merely claimed that Beckett's fiction suffers from the fallacy of expressive or imitative form; it collapses because its subject matter is the experience of collapsing:

In the novels Beckett yields progressively to the magnetic pull of the primitive, to the desire to achieve, by various forms of decadence and deformation, some Work that eludes the intellect, avoids the spread nets of habitual meaning.

But in a review of Beckett's *How It Is*, three or four years later, Frank found an adequate smidgeon of continuity:

This suggests that the delights offered by Beckett are of an old and tried variety. He has re-invented philosophical and theological allegory, and as surely as Spenser he needs the right to sound sub-rational, to conceal intention under an appearance of dreamlike fortuity, to obscure the literal sense. The only difference is that his predecessors were sure there was such a sense, and on this bitch of a planet he can no longer have such certainties.

The merit of these divergences and peculiarities is not merely that they show Frank's mind in transit, but that they impel his readers to do a good deal of thinking that wouldn't otherwise have occurred to us.

The thinking that Frank has been asking us to do, in his recent essays, arises from close work on particular passages in Shakespeare, Conrad and other writers. These essays – and Frank is pre-eminently an essayist, making forays and interventions – are timely. It is splendid to see him engaged with words, phrases, values impinging on other values in their contexts. He has always been a superb practical critic. Even when the occasion has required theoretical reflections, he has been visibly pleased to come to the particular book, the scene in the novel, as in 'Secrets and Narrative Sequence'. That started as a lecture in a conference on Narrative, but it turned into a remarkably telling commentary on several passages from *Under Western Eyes*. The commentary was not subdued to the motif of secrecy – nor was it subdued to that vocabulary in *The Genesis of Secrecy*. Razumov's confession to Natalia Haldin is studied on the understanding that it has rights beyond the expectations and vocabularies we bring to it. If we read it casually, much of it seems noise, but if we attend to it more responsibly we find its detail making 'another and rarer kind of sense'. The whole essay is exhilarating, it is like the sea at Brighton (as Olivier said of someone's performance in a great play).

Denis Donoghue

27. THE PLEASURES OF FRANKNESS

Oh how I grieve, that late born modesty
Hath got such root in easy waxen hearts,
That men may not themselves, their own good parts
Extol, without suspect of surquedry,
For, but thyself, no subject can be found
Worthy thy quill, nor any quill resound
Thy worth but thine; how good it were to see
A poem in thy praise, and writ by thee.

John Donne, 'To Mr T. W.'

IN THE MEMOIR *Not Entitled* – poetic, beautifully
written, and exquisitely moving though it is – Frank
Kermode assiduously avoids extolling his own good
parts or wielding his quill to re-sound his own substantial worth. Instead, readers find chapter headings such as
'Incomplete,' 'The Rest,' and 'Errors,' as well as persistent suggestions that any autobiography is condemned to
fail to tell the truth to the very degree that it is well written. Many of Frank's friends have drawn the following
obvious conclusion from this feature of the memoir:
Frank's best writing is about his weaknesses, lacks, failures, inadequacies; hence those portions of the autobiography must be those the farthest from the truth.

But the poignant conclusion of the memoir includes
one admission that squares perfectly with the man I came
to know as he was completing *Not Entitled* here in
Houston in early 1995. He wrote then that 'I have lacked
a place to be nostalgic about, but I've gone on hoping to
find one ... [with] a deity to command the perspective,
to appear each morning out of the dark or the mist, and
invite me to feel, as it were, presided over: a household
god or goddess to assure me that I was at home.' The
generous gift of the statue of Diana gives readers of the
memoir the sense of an appropriate fulfilment of that
desire, but Frank had moved himself and Diana almost

before the book was published, and she resides now not at the end of a long garden perspective but squeezed in front of a garage before a small condominium car park where vandals and thieves from time to time threaten her. Diana had offered and continues to offer something of an answer to Frank's need for a sense of home, but his continuing 'vague longing' for some kind of home seems to me still to evoke his best moments of writing and of friendship.

While longing for home, Frank often finds temporary shelter and comfort in the routine pleasures of exercise, eating, and drinking. We met in fact because his old friend Bob Patten found out that Frank was missing a regular squash match while in Houston for the first of three winter/spring terms at the University of Houston (one of them jointly at Rice), and Bob suggested that I call Frank. I did, and we settled into a pattern of twice or thrice weekly matches, often with Steven Crowell and Harvey Yunis, that were followed by gin and tonics, or beer at the Black Labrador, or, on special occasions (such as Fridays), by the driest coldest martinis in the world at Tony Mandola's restaurant. Seeing Frank take pleasure in such routines is itself such a pleasure that I even enjoy watching him indulge in one of his other great routine solaces, tobacco, and have felt a certain amount of envy for those who are willing to step outside for a smoke with Frank.

But the greatest pleasure of friendship with Frank comes with the conviction that for at least one other confessional moment in *Not Entitled* he told the truth about himself even though writing well: 'From poetry and music I derive the little I know about holiness,' the passage begins. To have the pleasure of watching Frank, pipe in hand, eyes shut tight, radiant with joy, as he listens to performances by artists such as Margaret Price, Teresa Stich-Randall, or Rene Fleming, whether live or recorded, whether of Mozart's *Zaide*, Handel's

Rodelinda, Strauss's *Four Last Songs*, Schubert's *Nacht und Träume*, or Frank's especial favorite, Bach's *Actus Tragicus*, is to share in the sense of art's sacredness and to know that, *pace* Keats, heard melodies are sweeter.

Quite recently, for the second time in several years, I renewed my sense of this special pleasure of watching Frank embrace the pleasures of music and verse at Tam and Chris Carlson's home in a place about which I am hopelessly nostalgic, Sewanee, Tennessee. Sewanee, location of The University of the South, is very different from what it was during my time there in the middle 1970s, and more different still from the time when the poet Allen Tate offered to bring Frank and his former wife over the Smokies by mule to the Mountain, or when Monroe Spears, longtime resident of Sewanee and editor of the *Sewanee Review*, wrote in 1970 in *Dionysus and the City* that 'Frank Kermode, the most important of these critics who reassert the claims of history and reason, is emphatically not the representative of any school. He avoids controversy and is suspicious of concern about critical method. His great virtue ... is his willingness to do any homework necessary to the full understanding of the work he is dealing with and then to submit himself to the work patiently and with full imaginative sympathy before trying to judge it' (p. 203). Sewanee nevertheless remains a place where such valuable and vivid voices as Frank's are accorded real attention and a genuine audience by a community with a rich sense of the values of art and of those who enable others to appreciate those values. On this trip, Frank, Tony Holden, my wife, Julie, and I went together from Nashville to see Frank receive formal recognition of Sewanee's appreciation for him, an honorary degree for his achievements in the world of letters. Though Frank's lecture while there and his appearance before a literary criticism class of Dale Richardson's were fine and valuable moments, as was conversation with George Core, present editor of the *Review*, and with others, those who did not see Frank rapt before the Carlson stereo speakers did not see Frank at his best, a picture of what all his texts have ultimately been, a model of respectful appreciation for the beautiful and the true and for their makers, and an image of someone who was, however fleetingly, completely at home.

Logan Browning

28. ROMANTIC IMAGE

I BORROWED Frank Kermode's *Romantic Image* soon after it was published in 1957 and was both impressed and puzzled by it. This brief but highly suggestive essay on the art, writing and theatrical events of the fin de siècle was tremendously interesting, but it did not fit my idea of what literary criticism should be like. At that time I accepted the assumption of the American New Critics, with added Scrutineering over-tones, that the object of literary attention should be the text in itself, a verbal icon or a well-wrought urn, with-out accretions. Frank's semi-Warburgian exploration of the cultural matrix of early modernism could not be fit-ted into that rather restrictive approach, but I was drawn to it despite my reservations. I was then a postgraduate at Oxford, where I had gone as a mature student in my mid-twenties to read English, following several years as a member of the white-collar proletariat in London, writ-ing poems and reviews after work. Academic life had come to seem very attractive after that existence and I was determined to stay in it, sending off applications for assistant lecturerships in English all over the country.

About this time I met Frank, probably through Ian Fletcher, a common acquaintance. Fletcher lived not far from me in Lewisham; he was a poet and an amateur scholar who knew an immense amount about the aesthetic movement and the fin de siècle. I have written about his original and striking personality in an article 'Friends from the Fifties' (*London Magazine*, February-March 1998), and there is a splendid account of him in Frank's memoir, *Not Entitled*. Frank was then a lecturer at Reading University, and he describes the complex manoeuvres by which he and Professor Donald Gordon translated Fletcher from his day job in a public library to a lecturership at Reading, despite his lack of paper qualifications.

I don't remember much about my first meeting with Frank, except that he came across as mild, amiable, friendly. Either on this occasion or at a later meeting he quietly gave me a piece of useful advice. I had applied for a post at Reading but had not been invited for interview. Frank had seen my papers and he recommended me to drop one of my referees in Oxford, who was not doing me any good. His reputation was then taking off with the growing celebrity of *Romantic Image*, which went into a second edition. The success of the book and Frank's other academic and literary activities meant that in 1958, at the age of thirty-eight, he was appointed Professor of English Literature at Manchester. This was good news for me, still sending off job applications, as it meant I had a friend at the top. Before long an assistant lecturership at Manchester was advertised. I applied, full of hope and confidence, and was invited to an interview. Frank was on the panel, as professor-elect, though he would not be in post until the autumn. I did not get the job, which was a considerable disappointment, though I could not really complain; the successful candidate, John Beer, a scholar of the Romantic period, was more experienced and better qualified than me. Years later he became a Professor at Cambridge.

A few days later, as I was recovering from my disappointment, I had a letter from Frank, saying he was sorry I had not got the job but there would be a similar post advertised the following year and he hoped I would apply for it, in, as he kindly put it, the unlikely event that I had not got a job by then. This was very encouraging to me, and represented an act of marked (though perhaps imprudent) good will on Frank's part. The months passed and I worked at my thesis on the early scientific romances of H.G.Wells, which I was treating as a fin de siècle topic, hence my interest in Frank's book. I still did not get a job. As a former mature student who contributed to little magazines and was working on an out-of-the-way subject I must have seemed a dubious prospect. Some time after the interview I met Frank who repeated his encouragement and remarked that in the eyes of the established academic world – and I imagine he had his fellow-professors at Manchester in mind – one scholarly article in the hard-nosed *Review of English Studies* was worth any amount of critical writing in literary journals. As it happened, in the course of my work on Wells I had become interested in the differences between the various texts of *The Time Machine*. I brushed up my knowledge of bibliography and produced an impeccably 'scholarly' essay on the complex publishing history of Wells's first novel. I submitted it to the *Review of English Studies*, which accepted it, to my hubristic satisfaction. Things, it seemed, were going my way, but not to the extent of securing me an academic post.

By the beginning of 1959 I was getting anxious. My research award from the state would come to an end in the summer and prospects were bleak, unless I had a breakthrough at Manchester. When an assistant lecturership there was advertised, I sent in my application, though I had a bad moment when an acquaintance in Oxford remarked, 'Oh, I heard that job has been fixed'. Could it have been fixed for me, I dared to wonder. Once more I travelled north and awaited my turn to be interviewed in the imposing, grimy, Gothic central building of Manchester University, the original Owen's College.

These days applicants for lecturerships have a painfully protracted wait after the interview before they know how they have fared, as no one is told anything until after the successful candidate has accepted in writing. Then it was simpler, at least at Manchester. After all the applicants had been interviewed an official called me in and I was offered the job. I gratefully accepted it and took the train back to Oxford, relieved and euphoric. I was thirty that year and in those days an academic job, no matter how lowly a start one made, was, if one kept one's nose clean, a job for life. Frank's support must have been crucial, though the forthcoming appearance of my article in the *RES* would have helped. Sometime after the interview I bought my own copy of *Romantic Image*, which I still have, bearing my signature and the date '1959'.

I taught at Manchester from 1959 to 1966, though Frank and I were together in the department for only part of that time. He had a year in America, then I did, in 1964–65, and when I got back he had departed to take a up a Chair at Bristol, in the next stage of the peregrination that subsequently led him to University College London, to Cambridge, and to Columbia. At Manchester we got on well, though friendship was sometimes affected by hierarchical considerations. Frank was head of department and my boss, and I was an ambitious over-age junior lecturer, and our relations were not always without institutional friction. But mostly they were genial. He invited me to contribute an essay to a collection on Milton that he was editing and I wrote a piece on the modern critical debates about Milton; I do not remember it with much affection; indeed barely remember it all, and I no longer have a copy of it, or even of the volume in which it came out, *The Living Milton*, published in 1960. When Frank's book of essays *Puzzles and Epiphanies* appeared in 1962 he acknowledged my assistance in the preface, though I don't think I did much

beyond advising on the selection of material and pointing out that the title of one of essays would serve well for
the whole collection. I recall irritating Frank by telling
him that the shortish review-article on Salinger was the
best thing he had done; it is a very good piece but that
was a perverse, perhaps provocative judgment on my
part.

In 1966, a year after Frank left Manchester, I moved
to Warwick. Our meetings thereafter were not frequent
but were warm when they occurred, and supported by
intermittent correspondence. His example meant a great
deal to me in my own career. Apart from his achievements in both Renaissance and modern scholarship, his
extensive literary journalism points the lesson that if one
is interested in literature, ideally one should be interested
in all of it, and in many other subjects too. An impossible ideal, of course, but 'a man's reach should exceed his
grasp ...' It would not go down well in the contemporary
academy, where the study of literature, like everything
else, is severely specialized and compartmentalized. Since
those Manchester days Frank has published a good many
books; most of them are on the Kermode shelf in my
study, some signed and inscribed by the author. I have
taken great pleasure in dedicating to him a forthcoming
book of my own, a collection of essays called *War Poets
and Other Subjects*.

Bernard Bergonzi

29. TENTATIVITIES AND INCONCLUSIONS

FRANK KERMODE is the most generous of critics,
not because he says flattering things about books
but because he listens to what they have to say. A
footnote in his first book, the Arden *Tempest*, exempli-
fies his whole career. Writing about the 'apparently triv-
ial allusions' to Dido and Aeneas in II.i, he concludes: 'It

is a possible inference that our frame of reference is badly adjusted, or incomplete, and that an understanding of this passage will modify our image of the whole play.' Books are voluble but reticent beings. They tell Frank more about themselves than they tell other critics because he never insists that they answer his private repertory of questions whether or not they care about them, and because he understands that the most interesting things that books have to say are answers they give to the questions that most readers are not sympathetic enough to ask.

Intimacy is a form of generosity. When Frank wrote *Romantic Image* in the mid-1950s, most writers about Modernism genuflected to T. S. Eliot as the one infallible authority on literature and history. Frank recognised that the 'dissociation of sensibility' (which Eliot had perceived in the period around 1650) had never happened, and that Eliot's version of history issued from deep personal nostalgia. Frank was too tactful to mention that sensibility had dissociated itself at almost the precise moment when Eliot's ancestors left England for America, but Eliot and many of his readers would have needed no reminder. *Romantic Image* had almost nothing respectful to say about Eliot, but understanding is more gratifying than respect, and the book was the first step in Eliot's transformation in the public eye from a remote impersonal sage to a tormented human soul. In the same way, his disrespectful but attentive book on D. H. Lawrence outraged true-believing Lawrentians, but it explained Lawrence and his work more persuasively than anyone else had done.

Frank's tact is evident throughout his work. Almost uniquely among critics, he observes the peculiarities and quiddities of a book without feeling tempted to generalise or moralise about them. His essay on the secrets half-revealed in *Under Western Eyes* is typical of his method. The essay deploys a series of theoretically subtle techniques to trace a network of links between the diction and structure of the novel and such mundane matters as Conrad's finances and publishing history, and, as it does so, it seems to be building towards a theoretical generalisation about literature and life that never arrives. This is the same method found on a larger scale in *The Genesis of Secrecy*. In each case, the experience of reading Frank is salutary and unsettling: the reader who wants to be taught a method – a technique to apply with minimal effort to any book that happens to be under scrutiny – is taught instead that theoretical sophistication is the starting point of criticism, not its goal. For all his magisterial capaciousness and authority, Frank often seems tentative and inconclusive, and his work is all the better for it. Because he values the uniqueness of literary works, he knows they are misused when they are discussed as if they existed in order to confirm someone's general ideas, especially his own. 'No theory, no history', was a motto cited approvingly by Fernand Braudel, who also understood that the history was the point and purpose of the theory.

A conventional scene in movie westerns is the barroom brawl in which drunken cowboys smash balsa-wood tables over each other's heads while the hero, holding the hand of the beautiful schoolmarm, navigates his unruffled way to the exit. This scene accurately portrays Frank's relation to the vexed field of literary theory. Those critics who apply one master-theory to every book invariably get entangled in angry battle for supremacy with other critics with competing master-theories. Frank, in contrast, regards all theories as potentially useful instruments of interpretation, and walks away from the balsa-wood battles of the theoreticians with new methods that he can try out on books to see if they respond.

No theory is alien to him, but none commands his servitude. The genius of his criticism is his ability to find among the babble of competing theories the one that speaks most clearly and directly with whatever book he is writing about.

'It is possible that our frame of reference is badly adjusted.' Frank recognised that this possibility applies not only to individual works but also to whole periods of literary history. In his reviews and essays in the early 1980s he began remarking in an offhand way that Modernism would look different if people bothered to read Arnold Bennett's *Riceyman Steps*, a novel of astonishing complexity and depth that was entirely unlike the canonical classics of the 1920s. Readers who took Frank's hint and read an out-of-print copy of Bennett's novel typically felt the historical ground shifting under their feet as the great twentieth-century classics moved to new and more plausible positions. Characteristically, Frank was too tactful to point out that the standard history of Modernism had been built on the absurdities and lies promulgated by Ezra Pound, and that the whole story must someday be written anew. But Frank's small gestures, like praise for a forgotten novel, may do more than any massive polemics to overturn the Potemkin villages of conventional literary history.

Major critics, as they grow older, become increasingly interested in two things: the Bible, and their personal relation to the books they write about. These two tendencies are perhaps separate expressions of one impulse towards relationship. The Bible is a book about the relations of individual nations, individual human beings and an individual God, relations that take the form of promises, covenants, and similar matters of conscience and commitment. Frank's best books are his most recent, least fashionable, and most personal ones. *History and*

Value interprets books written in the 1930s from a breathtakingly complex set of perspectives: how they looked to Frank when he first read them; how they look to him fifty years later; how they looked to their authors; and how they alter the shape of critical theory and literary history by being remembered now. *An Appetite for Poetry* declares in its title the personal commitment of its author; the book itself starts in an unabashedly 'apologetic mode'; and it ends with chapters on the Bible.

In the early 1980s Frank spent a few semesters at Columbia University after his retirement from Cambridge. He came to an English department that had long been a breeding ground for competitive furies. Many of its members seemed most concerned with the relative opulence of their offices and the relative number of departmental responsibilities they could avoid performing. One anti-imperialist professor proposed to knock down the wall between her office and an adjacent one so that she could usurp the territory that had been settled for decades by a hapless colleague. Another crusader for the downtrodden refused to read graduate-student applications and asserted that his lesser-known colleagues should do the job for him; he only dropped the idea when the department secretary told him he would have to explain this to them personally. Frank, by demanding nothing for himself, set an example that almost revived the golden age. He seemed not to notice that his office was small and his desk rickety, but sat down at the battered typewriter provided for him and wrote his luminous essays. He regularly attended dull committee meetings and, although he was in residence only half the year and was not expected to evaluate graduate theses or prospective faculty, performed every task with a quiet competence that shamed the irresponsible. Within a day after his departure, the iron age resumed.

Has any critic earned so much personal gratitude in the course of a career that he himself seems to regard as a fiasco of wrong moves? Readers of *Not Entitled* watch helplessly, shouting 'Don't do it, Frank', as the author ponders yet another disastrous personal or professional move, only to make that move on the very next page. Yet the book itself, like everything Frank has written, is its own triumph, a masterpiece of lucidity and depth, an oasis of calm in the midst of its disturbances.

A secular teacher who creates disciples fails, because the task of a teacher is to help students learn their own autonomy and obligations. Frank inspires admiration and affection in thousands of intelligent readers, but perhaps the most significant tribute to his teaching is the fact that there are no Kermodians. Officialdom for once got it right when his name appeared in the Honours List; his friends and readers had known him for years to be a very perfect gentle knight.

Edward Mendelson

30. THE WRITER LIVES ON

WHEN EVERYMAN'S LIBRARY was relaunched in 1990 and I found myself installed in the editorial chair, I knew we were going to need all the help we could get. The Library is a cultural monument over which my most celebrated predecessor, Ernest Rhys, reigned for almost forty years. Though Everyman went into decline during the 1960s, Rhys and his successors had built up a remarkable reputation for the Library and there was a great deal to live up to.

The first step was to establish an editorial board, and the first person to approach for membership was obviously Frank Kermode - 'obviously' because he is self-evidently the most distinguished figure in English literary studies. What Graham Greene said about Evelyn Waugh is what writers, teachers, critics and editors might now say about Frank: he is the head of our profession.

This very distinction made me cautious. He must be a busy man, he might be a formidable one. As an Oxonian, my limited view of English at Cambridge also suggested that its practitioners were by inclination severe, remote, controversial and unyielding. Reputedly, they breathe a finer air in the Fens than the mists of the Thames valley. I need not have worried. From the start, Frank was enthusiastic, sympathetic, friendly and endlessly helpful. If my telephone calls and letters come at awkward moments, he never betrays the fact, and he always has the answers to my questions.

His legendary tolerance was tested early on in our relationship when I asked him to lunch with another Everyman contributor, Michael Foot, but failed to put a proper sign on the door of our scruffy office, then in Berwick Street above a sex shop. A colleague spied Michael through the window and escorted him upstairs, but there was no sign of Frank. Arriving in Soho from Cambridge, he had been quite unable to find us and went home without his lunch. Imagining the reactions of certain distinguished academics I know under similar circumstances and realising the debacle was entirely my fault, I trembled for the future, but Frank characteristically blamed himself, adding, 'It does me good to miss lunch occasionally.' The modesty and lack of egotism apparent in his work, where opinions take second place to scholarship and rational argument, are equally conspicuous in his professional life, even – perhaps especially – when dealing with his juniors.

This sympathy for others seems to me Frank's distinguishing characteristic, both as a scholar and as a man. Working outside the academic world, I have been especially struck by his rapport with writers. Anyone who knows his books knows that he has rare critical intelligence and erudition, the gift for going straight to the point and a formidable grasp of literary theory – not only the fashionable stuff of recent years, but the very notion of literature as an intellectual domain. Yet one always feels that he is most at home with writing as a craft and an art. Unlike many critics, he is sensitive to writers as people, human beings making – or not making – sense out of the world. The author may be dead, but in Frank's thinking the writer lives on.

I became acutely aware of this on my all too rare visits to King's where hospitality and conversation are dispensed with equal generosity. A particular pleasure on these occasions was the presence of Frank's friend and colleague, the late Tony Tanner, whom I and David Campbell got to know well. With his encyclopaedic knowledge and huge enthusiasm, Tony was equally alert to the writer's role and the interrelation of writing and criticism. Listening to them both talk was, as they say, an education in itself: warm, brilliant, amusing, informed, always candid but always liberal.

It was Frank who helped to make possible Tony's contribution to the Everyman Library, in particular his magisterial introductions to the seven volumes of the complete plays of Shakespeare which occupied much of his time in the last years of his life. I know that Tony himself regarded these introductions as his greatest achievement. They are shortly to be published in one volume, which will, in its way, be a testament to Frank's care for a dear friend.

Peter Washington

5

ISLANDER

31. THE ISLANDER

THE FIRST MESSAGE of Frank Kermode's *Not Entitled* – the principal thing he seems to wish to tell the world – is 'I am an islander.' As with so many good autobiographies, the part dealing with childhood is the best. The later parts, recounting various academic clashes and tensions (in which a love of red-brick and a converse deep mistrust of Oxbridge are discernible) are both expert and instinct with a sort of intellectual passion, but the great thing is the Isle of Man, which did what islands do. It insulated.

It is tempting to see Frank's insular *Bildung* as contributing to his later insight into the Renaissance fascination with microcosms and macrocosms, with the little world within each of us as a reflection of the larger world of sun, moon, stars, earth, animals, vegetables, minerals. For Frank the little world – not of man but of Man – was the source of an initial deprivation, but a special sort of deprivation which could be set right, spectacularly, through the availability of books. If the Isle of Man was a prison it was nevertheless all windows. My own memories of the weekly arrival in our remote Herefordshire village of the circulating library van suggest a fainter version of the same thing. One senses that without the initial cultural starvation Frank might not have read as gluttonously as he obviously did. The island became a transparent sphere of words in which all cultures, all literatures shone through from outside.

But then came Frank's bodily translation from the island to the mainland, from obscurity to complex, brilliant academic performance in the larger world. This record of public performance implies an immense inner facility. The word 'facility' has a disparaging ring, but I intend no disparagement by it here, only admiration. Frank has had problems in his academic life but they all appear, very clearly, to impact upon him from outside. He seems to have no trouble in knowing, discriminating, thinking and writing well. He has done everything: criticism, theory, reviewing, literary journalism and the most demanding kind of editing, over an extraordinary historical range. The real weight lifted seems inconsistent with the ease with which the thing was done. We instinctively mistrust feats achieved without stumbling or hesitation, but we ought not to; in fact the feat is thereby all the greater.

Consider his introductory essays to the Tragedies in the *Riverside Shakespeare*. There was a great responsibility here. This was to become the collected Shakespeare in the hands of large numbers of students in this country and vast numbers in the United States, for many years to come. This would, for good or ill, 'set' minds. More than a quarter of a century – in which much has happened in Shakespearian criticism – has passed since these introductions were written, but the effortless mastery with which nail after nail is knocked on the head remains startling. When Frank calls Coriolanus 'an ugly political innocent' one catches one's breath that four words can say so much. The rebarbative awfulness of Coriolanus, his brutal contempt for the people, are there in the first epithet; then the theoretical implications of this play, which have engrossed the politically minded from Hazlitt to Brecht and after, are there in the second; then, best of all, comes the word 'innocent' – Coriolanus's deeply pitiable, disastrous childlikeness. Near the end of the play it is the word 'boy' which calls forth his most terrifying display of rage. Yet Frank's phrasing is elegantly smooth, makes no parade of intricacy or difficulty. So it is throughout the *Riverside* introductions. When he writes of *Romeo and Juliet*, 'The reality of the love relationship is even, by a touch of genius, contrasted with the relative falsity even of the grief of parents', some might say that there is here a danger of crowding too many thoughts into one proposition (the expertly concessive second 'even' breaks into the thought at the very last moment) but in fact the sentence holds its cadence and makes its admirably subtle point. Frank puts no inverted commas round the word 'reality' (a practice which has become almost *de rigueur* since the 1970s) but this does not, now, come across as old-fashioned. It is oddly refreshing.

As one reads through these brief essays one can watch the writer thinking – a little harder each time he returns to the theme – about time. Of course by this date he had already written *The Sense of an Ending* and more – much more – was to follow. Like many before him he finds retarded action in *Hamlet* but like few he goes on to find a precisely converse acceleration in *Othello*, before he launches into his swift analysis of the notorious 'double time-scheme' (Desdemona has two days of married life with Othello yet she can plausibly be represented by Iago as having been habitually unfaithful to her husband). Always, Frank thinks simultaneously of the pressures exerted within the work of art by dramatic plotting and the like and also of larger modes of causation. The latter line of thought reaches a kind of climax in one marvellous observation: 'The suffering of the Macbeths may be thought of as caused by the pressure of the world of order slowly assuming its true shape and crushing them.' To those who know the play the sentence is strong because it carries, implicitly, a memory of the play's recurrent imagery of bodies which are the wrong size for their garments:

> He cannot buckle his distemper'd cause
> Within the belt of rule ...
>   Now does he feel his title
> Hang loose about him, like a giant's robe
> Upon a dwarfish thief ...

But Frank takes the image and runs with it. I have no

idea what the real sequence of thought was but cannot help guessing that his mind passed from 'buckle' in the sense 'fasten' to the other sense 'cave in' (one can watch this happening to the word in Hopkins's 'The Wind-hover') but then he moves from Macbeth buckling under the strain to the opposite of caving in, to the idea of a robust structure whch slowly reverts to its former shape and size. But this reversion is, horribly, at the expense of the Macbeths. Even the phrase, 'the Macbeths', which may strike the ignorant as inappropriately bourgeois, is spot on. No play of Shakespeare shows a more intimate marriage than this one. Despite the title the tragedy belongs to both husband and wife. As the old Puritans used to say, Frank Kermode is 'inward' with the writings of Shakespeare.

Aponos kathupertatos allon, 'without labour superior to the rest'. The words are from a Greek poem which Robert Levens, classics tutor at Merton College, Oxford, produced in honour of the eightieth birthday of the English scholar H. W. Garrod. Levens told me that he was trying to express in Greek the cant phrase of the time, 'the effortless superiority of the Balliol man'. Of course all that lordly nonsense about Balliol men is pro-foundly at odds with everything Frank stands for, but 'effortless superiority' is right. This alone, to some, will always be a species of offence. I once had to introduce a lecture by Frank and I racked my brains for a single, summarising word to describe him. I wanted to avoid the vaguely Leavisite suggestion of judgement as the central activity, a suggestion which lurks in terms like 'critic' and 'discrimination'. I ended by using the gauche word 'understander'. Frank understands literature better than anyone I can think of.

The autobiography cannot, because it is sane and just, apologise for Frank's brilliance but it does offer a kind of counterbalance. Certainly he must always have been clever. But at the same time he was, he tells us, fat, unprepossessing and amazingly clumsy with (as it might be) rewiring an electric plug. Given the unbroken grace and elegance of Frank's prose, it may well come as a comfort to the rest of us that he, of all people, could be clumsy, in any department of life. I can believe that Frank was – perhaps still is – physically clumsy. I find it harder to believe that he was ever unprepossessing. The man I know has always been, whenever we have met, a quiet, charming, noticeably personable figure. One invariably feels slightly gross, standing beside him, or speaking after he has just spoken.

A. D. Nuttall

32. TRYING TO BE FRANK

IN THE 1930S many a literary career was launched in one or other of the 'little magazines'. So it was with Frank Kermode, who first attracted critical acclaim with a piece in one such little magazine, *The Cushag*.

Not a lot of people know this, oddly enough. Come to that, not a lot of people know that *The Cushag* was (pity about the *was*) the house journal of Douglas High School, or indeed that *cushag* is a shortened form of Manx *cuishag vooar*, meaning 'big stalk'. There may even be people who – despite the loving references to it in the voluminous writings of Hall Caine – don't know that the cushag is the Manx floral emblem, as precious to the hearts in Ellan Vannin as cherry blossom to those in Japan. True, the little yellow flower is a modest affair, and you'll have noticed that even the Manx name itself refers only to the stalk (big, mind you; size matters) and not to the bloom itself. So no one in the Isle of Man pretends that the cushag should be heralded like the fleur-de-lys or cosseted like the orchid. But equally none of us can be other than miffed at the way the *OED*, with that smug hauteur we associate with Oxford, dismisses it as 'common ragwort', with a citation expressly classifying it as a weed. No wonder Frank and I grew up to feel Oxbridge coolly distant and more than a little snooty.

I say 'Frank and I' familiarly, but there was no great familiarity between us at school. True, we both wrote for *The Cushag* as did contemporaries like Nigel Kneale, though not everything in that worthy little mag was likely to raise Manx brows from low to middling. But there was little else by way of extracurricular activity to bring Frank and me together. Being a year younger can create quite a gulf when you're in your early teens. Besides, he was the model pupil, his name on every teacher's lips as a goal for the rest of us – forlornly – to aspire to. So, a year behind him in time, I watched Frank from a respectful distance, properly conscious of being immeasurably below him in intellect. And just as, in the nature of things, I never caught up with him temporally, so I never (as Frank would be the first to agree) caught up with him intellectually. Not for want of trying. Nor for want of encouragement. 'Why can't you write a bit more like Kermode?' 'Widen your reading like Kermode.' 'Kermode has set a record for exam distinctions: just you try and get close!' 'Kermode read that in a couple of nights' ('that' being variously *Paradise Lost*, *Buddenbrooks*, *The Fairie Queene*, *War and Peace*, or some little *roman fleuve* like *A la recherche du temps perdu*). Terrifying of course, and not the sort of thing that necessarily endears a chap to his mates, especially as such bookwormly achievements were far from the targets on which most kids set their sights, like sport and sex. But at least it instilled a certain respect.

I was just close enough behind him in school to get the full impact of all this. It was like being a dinghy in the wake of a battle cruiser doing thirty knots; there's no chance of catching up, but some chance of sharing the exhilaration if you're not sunk without trace.

We had no contact during the war, he in the Navy, I in the Air Force (each in our small way giving added reason for gloom in anyone contemplating the words 'When Britain stood alone'), and even afterwards, both on our way up an academic pole that was far less greasily hazardous then than now, we met only sporadically. But I took good care to read his every word and I kept on trying ... We got our first chairs in the same year, his in Manchester, mine in Durham, and within a decade I was in a position to organise the process of enticing him to Bloomsbury as Northcliffe Professor in succession to James Sutherland.

'Northcliffe Professor of Literature?' sneered a cynic when the chair was established in the Thirties. 'As well endow a Mammon Chair of Divinity!' Maybe something in this *mot* caught Frank's fancy because it was certainly during his years at UCL that he developed his interest in hermeneutics and reread the Gospels with theological devotion.

Happy days! At that time, the two senior professors, Quain (me) and Northcliffe (him), were obliged by regulation to be joint heads of department, a recipe that might have been specially designed to provoke conflict. But it never happened with us. There was nary a cloud to darken our sky as we busily wrote, taught – yes, and innovated. This was the time of worldwide student unrest: death at Kent State, gas at Berkeley, barricades in Paris, mayhem in Berlin and turmoil everywhere. But in UCL's English Department the turmoil was largely cerebral, as teachers and students engaged in constructive (if seemingly interminable) dialogue from which emerged a radically new syllabus, teaching style and examining system.

This was also the time when 'interdisciplinary thinking' was all the rage, finding synergies between philosophy, anthropology, visual and mental perception, linguistic and literary theory, brushing aside the barriers between science and the humanities discussed and some-what exaggerated by C. P. Snow. The wiring at UCL provided some particularly valuable circuitry. During Frank's years in the College, some of our more active 'interdisciplinary' colleagues included J. Z. Young, Alex Comfort, Bill Coldstream, Leo Ettlinger, John Hale, Michael Halliday, Mary Douglas, Richard Wollheim, Peter Stern, Jonathan Miller (with his in-law Karl just down the road), Mary Wilkinson, and Noel Annan in the Provost's office, plus Joe Trapp and Ernst Gombrich a few yards away in the Warburg.

All intensely stimulating (and not just intellectually: witness Bel Mooney and Jonathan Dimbleby). Not for the first time, or the last, Bloomsbury was a-buzz. And it was a buzz in which Frank and I revelled. I recall crowded weekly seminars where staff and graduate students from widely different academic patches – critics, medievalists, grammarians – not only learned each other's engagement and mode of 'discourse' (as we were already calling it) but confidently challenged each other too. Yes, and even challenged the VIP visitors we welcomed from time to time. Such as Roland Barthes. In French. And as this implies, those seminars were not just parochial English department affairs; interested people from other departments joined in and I recall Annette Lavers as a particularly valued regular. What's more, the English department broadened its interests in other notable ways. How could it be otherwise when, adding to the breadth already provided by dons as different as Basil Greenslade and John Dodgson, we were able to corral such new recruits as Rosemary Ashton, Antonia Byatt, David Daniell, Stephen Fender, Michael Mason, John Sutherland, Sarah Wintle and, of course, Stephen Spender?

It was all (though it shouldn't have been) too good to last. In 1974, to the deep regret of his London friends and – as it quickly turned out – to his own as well, Frank left to become the King Edward VII Professor of English Literature in Cambridge.

Now, it's understandably hard for a humble (or formerly humble or formally humble) grammar-school product to resist (if I may so calque the German *Ruf*) a 'call' to Oxbridge. And it's especially hard to make your very first landing in those arcane collegiate realms at professorial level, with snipers already at you while you're still wriggling out of the parachute harness. In 1980 I had an agonising struggle with just such an option myself, but being knowledgeably and convincingly warned that I'd be miserable in Oxford, I stayed put. Frank also agonised and was just as knowledgeably warned that if he left Bloomsbury for Cambridge he'd hate it, but he did and he did. He took the road less travelled by and that, as the man said, has made all the difference.

It has certainly made all the difference to any chance of my travelling with Frank ever since; indeed, we scarcely see each other these days. I still read pretty well everything he writes, of course. He remains the model he was set up to be during our school days. And I don't stop trying.

Randolph Quirk

33. PARALLELS AND PARADOXES: THE STORY OF A LITERARY FRIENDSHIP

HE LAUGHS GOOD-NATUREDLY at a tradesman's letter starting 'Dear Sir Kermode', but is genuinely annoyed if people pronounce him commode. It's the Manx version of McDermott, he says with quiet pride, the stress should be on the first syllable. Yet he left the Isle of Man as a young man and felt an outsider even then, as on later visits. He is, like most of us, a pack of paradoxes, but of very special paradoxes.

Is there any other author, for instance, who doesn't list his previous books on the flyleaf of each publication, or who (in Debrett's *People of Today*) lists the eight universities he taught in and the seven honorary doctorates he was awarded, but only five of his books (under the rubric 'author of numerous works, including ...')? Anyone can write 'numerous' books, he seems to say, but posts and honours are rarer. True.

Not quite. In the only other such surrogate of *Who's Who* I stupidly thought might be useful and isn't, the American *Who's Who in the World*, he has the same order, the same 'author of numerous books' but lists at least eleven. Still not all, but more balanced with the honours. For of course it's the questionnaires sent by these many surrogates which seem to be addressed to people with loads of honours and no books, giving much space for the former and very little for the latter. Such reference books stress the life not the communication, let alone the hoped-for afterlife. The latter goes into *Who Was Who*, by which time posts and ranks and honours are forgotten. In principle, often by pure canonic chance, the books (or one or two) survive, but this is less and less true, indeed they're more usually forgotten from decade to decade during the author's lifetime. All the media stress is on the present fame, usually of people who don't write books but get written about, presidents and other pundits. Which is odd because history, which used to be mostly about kings, their heirs, their rivals and their battles, now barely mentions them. Living in France, and retired, I wanted to brush up my history of France a few years ago and bought Duby's splendid production in three large illustrated volumes. I wanted it popular, history as remembered, and the pictures did occasionally show a person, king or captain or monk or mayor. But the text was mostly about economics and demography, from the thirteenth century on. The Annals school has been important of course, but does tend to sacrifice individuals.

So perhaps Frank is right to defend posts and honours in a world where these get so subsumed, and to leave the books to chance posterity, like bottles to the sea. I'm fiddling with the question because I've never had to think about it before. It's true that other entries, by authors who list endless books, are unreadable, but then such directories are not meant to be readable. It's also true that my own posts and honours are very skimpy indeed in comparison with his, but even those few I tend to omit, and were they as fulsome as his I would still stress the books. Just as I stress the text and not the author in criticism. But then so does he.

The author situation however is still more complex. We both went through schools of criticism that emphasised the text in some way or another, from the Twenties to the Sixties. Before that it was all 'author's intention' that counted (establish the author's intention and then judge whether he has realised it, a teacher's dictum still valid in Oxford in the late Forties, despite the then 'New' Criticism). And from those pre-Twenties days some myth of the author's biographical importance survived and dragged on in the reviewer's world against all that newfangled obsession with the text.

Then in the Sixties Barthes and Foucault announced the death of the author. This was of course a theoretical construct (or destruct) to do with narrative technique. Booth had brought out his 'Implied Author' and his variously qualified narrators. Very quickly the word 'author', now taboo, was quite simply replaced, in serious criticism, by the word 'narrator', thus confusing all instances in a meaningless ragbag. Indeed I'm always astonished by the docility with which serious critics follow the latest fads: as the critical fashions moved round Jakobson's diagram of communication from Author to Text to World to Reader the phrases merely altered from 'the author means' to 'the text says' to 'the reader infers', concealing the true proposition which is always 'I the critic think/guess/decide/proclaim ...'

Meanwhile the 'real' author has come back with a vengeance, with, if successful, interviews, invitations to read from and lecture on his work, to explain, to promote, to be starified. Win prizes. Honours. Posts. Is this critically or creatively wise? Interviews with authors are about as interesting as a tennis-player's clichés on how he won a match. Or, when the author does try to explain what she/he has been 'really' trying to do (i.e. in the text), nobody takes the slightest notice. What people want is cliché plot summary, cliché character-summary, cliché author-summary. Not even 'author of numerous books including'.

So Frank is right to stress that author. He is truly Entitled (see just below).

In fact we have curiously parallel lives, though in shifted times: both arriving in England as alien adolescents (from Man, from Brussels), learning more or less painfully how to behave in the middle-class English way and not always succeeding, frequently feeling a little out of place, *Not Entitled* (as his memoir is ironically called), each with two more or less happy but failed marriages, each becoming professors (he much earlier), though in very different ways and places, each a frequent guest professor in the States and elsewhere, even if he has attained far higher places and wider fame than I. And both reaching old age in serene and chosen solitude, each respecting the other's.

I even learned, from later acquaintance and from his memoir, that he had been a student in Liverpool before he joined the Navy when the war came, whereas I missed running him over by two years as I cycled down from West Derby, past the university and the foundations of the new Catholic cathedral, into the city as office girl at sixteen and seventeen in the first two years of the war, hating accountancy and joining the Air Force as soon as

I was eighteen. He says he 'wasted' six years of his life sailing round the world, whereas my four years of war, mostly at Bletchley Park, reading the whole war from the enemy viewpoint, surrounded with very clever intellectuals, was to me like a first university. My second (or first real one) was Oxford, just after the war, where I was anguished and disappointed with both its framework notions and its unpractical methods of teaching, so ill adapted to ex-Service students, after the rigourous standards of my warwork. But at least I went on to University College London for my doctorate, where I was given slightly more adequate attention by my supervisor (who, however, assumed I was doing it for fun before producing a family and never sent me up for job interviews, as he did the boys: we forget now how late prejudices were accepted as natural and correct).

Chiasmically he, at the other end of his career, after seven red-brick and black-brick but much more rigorous universities, was, as he himself acknowledges in *Not Entitled*, unable to resist the rags-to-riches top-notch offer of a Regius Chair in Cambridge, and left his 'real' chair at University College for this empty honour. And he too was bitterly disappointed by the framework notions and practical methods of teaching there, indeed, to the point of eventual and courageous resignation.

Despite these time-jerked parallels, we did not become friends till much later, though we came across each other early. He insists that we first met in the late Fifties, at a literary party in Islington, whereas I am sure it was at the American Embassy where he was lecturing on Wallace Stevens for USIS and I went up to him afterwards to congratulate him. Such is memory. His memoir mentions, *en passant*, other elements of the Fifties I was much concerned with, such as George Fraser's poetry parties. But from hearsay, for he never came, at least not when I did.

In fact my first contact with him, distant and literary, was inauspicious. I had just published *A Grammar of*

Metaphor in 1958 (a rewritten PhD thesis of 1954), but unlike him, could find no job in academia: as the refusals said, I was too qualified for the lowly ones but if I tried further up, lacked teaching experience. So I drifted into literary journalism, at first for the now defunct *Time and Tide*. There I reviewed Frank's second book, *Romantic Image* (1957), rather badly it seems: for Ian Fletcher, then a colleague of his at Reading but presumably encountered at George Fraser's in London, told me I had made a big mistake which I would long regret, since the author was a coming man, who would rise to great power. As a beginner, I had as yet no notion of power, and had no doubt naively 'said what I thought'. As far as I remember my review contained only one criticism, which I was inordinately proud of being able to make, scolding the author the way beginners do, for following the fashion and using the word 'image' to cover metaphor, simile, comparison, symbolic use and even literal evocation. This of course may not have been true, and I can't check, as this is one of the few books of Frank's I don't have, for poor reviewers sold all review copies then. Whatever the case, he never mentioned it, either at the Islington party I can't remember or at the US Embassy congratulation he can't (and which may have been earlier, since his book on Stevens was earlier).

The many books that came after that one were all much more exciting to me than the Romantics or their use of image. I had already enjoyed the Wallace Stevens (I was then plunged in Pound), but from *The Sense of an Ending* (1967) on, it was all astonishment and delight. What I admired and envied above all, apart from each its originality of theme and approach, was the quiet tone, the elegance, the discreet irony in which that originality was wrapped, and, above all, the apparently easy access through deceptively simple propositions that soon turned out to have been subtly enticing and exciting all the time, without oneupmanship, without bullying, but, quite surprisingly as I now nostalgically realise, in a gentle, well-mannered way. Wrapped, that is, in civilised, not vulgar, readability.

This last quality continued, however difficult the topic (such as, for instance, in *The Genesis of Secrecy*, 1979, the Greek word *hoti* in St Matthew's Gospel, implying an exclusion of some Christians as opposed to others). The ability to generate a whole book, a whole spray of problems, out of one Greek word not much noticed for 2,000 years (unless by theologians, specialists in the art of niggling), was immensely satisfying, I hope to him but certainly to his readers. This ability continued, moreover, throughout the Structuralist and Post-Structuralist fashions, which at their worst produced such a ludicrously jargonesque style, oneupmanship (or oneupwomanship alas). Nevertheless both these movements, it now seems for the last time, stressed the text, not the author. It's true that Structuralism emphasised abstract structure rather than concrete text (and, indeed, one or two Structuralists I could name would work from summaries). But structure is part of Form, not Content. The How, not the What. And Post-Structuralism, notably Deconstruction, was and is very text-orientated: indeed close reading is essential to demonstrate that a text purporting to say one thing is surreptitiously saying the opposite.

Frank went on as before, facing the new fashions with eager curiosity but refusing to drown in them. There are not many such eclectic, widely read yet deeply scholarly critics today whom I can read with such unannoyed pleasure.

Time, just on its inexorable own, seems to solidify friendships irrespective of meetings. For in fact we seldom met. Our lives were in different worlds. My husband taught at the School of Slavonic Studies (where his career had to endure the anti-foreign prejudices of the time), and I nowhere (for parallel prejudices). We were very poor. Frank was by then heading a department at

Manchester University, or maybe Bristol, and way out of ken. But he too reviewed. Still, we never reviewed each other (I reviewed chiefly novels, or else Pound books or French books for the *TLS*, or jazz books for *Time and Tide*). I do remember him praising a Spanish translation of mine, calling me 'the omnicompetent Miss Brooke-Rose'. So Ian Fletcher's prediction had not materialised. Indeed, as a publisher's reader Frank, unknown to me, twice gave me an excellent report. The first, linking me to French contemporary writing, was for my difficult (and I think best) novel *Thru* , in 1975, was very relevant to that book, but unfortunately a puff from it was repeated on the cover of almost every novel since, and probably did me much harm in the parochial English atmosphere. That of course is hardly his fault, and I was personally very proud of the quote. The second came much later, in the early Nineties, for my last critical book, *Stories, Theories and Things* (1991), by which time of course we had been meeting regularly, in Provence, London or Cambridge. I was and am still very grateful. I feel 'not entitled' after that early 'bad' review. But I know I helped him in other ways: when he needed to talk, at the unpleasant breakdown of his second marriage, I listened. Literary relationships aren't necessarily tit-for-tat; after all, his publishers never asked me for a report so I couldn't puff back. Otherwise, for many years, we were just printed names to each other.

In 1971, after I had been teaching at Paris-Vincennes for three years, I did go and see him at University College, London, where he was by then reigning, to see if there might be a job (I was still trying to repair a broken marriage, and couldn't get a regular job in England). There wasn't. But our real friendship probably started then. We met again at a party given by Faber, or rather by its chairman Peter du Sautoy and his wife Mollie, for my Pound book. Frank had asked me to bring him the latest number of *Tel Quel* ('*Roland Barthes par lui-*

même'), which I handed to him in front of the literary editor of the *Sunday Times*, for whom I used to write, who said 'ho-ho, the new theology, what!'

That was the atmosphere in London, the reflex attitude towards the interesting (if also smug and often pretentious) developments in Paris. I remember a small dinner several years later, around 1976, given by my other publisher with two well-known novelists. I had kept quiet, since everyone was talking of who had reviewed what where, and when asked what I thought I said I had no idea since I hadn't read the papers in question. This was met with incredulity, as for a delinquent foreigner, so I tried to explain that it was all I could do to read the latest Barthes or the latest Derrida. Who? Well (embarrassed, and to get it over fast), Structuralism and Post-Structuralism (for yes, they were contemporary, despite the later 'Post'). 'Oh,' said one of the novelists with audible relief, 'is Structuralism over? Oh, good.'

Frank was never like that, even in those days, but then nor was he ever like those many deriders who rush in where some (at least) Angles fear to tread; and even less like one eager-beaver who, blinded perhaps by what seemed to him a startling new discovery, came over to Paris and earnestly explained Roman Jakobson's diagram of communication to a vast conference of Structuralist and Post-Structuralist experts. Even I had been teaching such things to first-year students for some time, and squirmed for my countryman.

Frank was sophisticated enough to know that new critical systems inevitably have their flaws, even their aberrations, but that to speak of them with any degree of seriousness it is necessary to have gone through them, to understand them, to have worked them through texts. As with close reading of the text: *Forms of Attention* (the title of yet another of his 'numerous' books, 1985). In the case of both Structuralism and, *a fortiori*, Post-Structuralism, it was necessary not only to learn modern linguistics but to go back to Saussure (for Post-Structuralism), and (for Structuralism) to the Russian Formalists of the 1920s and to study their descendants Bakhtin and Lotman, as well as their even more modern descendants in France such as Todorov and Kristeva and, much less directly descendant, the philosophers Derrida and Deleuze and others.

And that is what he did. His famous seminar at University College (from, I think, 1971 to when he left for Cambridge) became famous precisely as the only one in Britain then where minds were being opened to what was going on in France, in Germany, in the US and elsewhere, and to attract speakers from all over. I attended it myself with great delight in 1972 when, in another vain attempt to mend my broken marriage, I spent a semester in London, commuting fortnightly to Vincennes.

It is important to understand other schools of criticism, to learn from their insights while rejecting their aberrations. I was raised on the New Criticism (not, however, at Oxford but alone), as presumably Frank was, and however attacked it later was for its elitism, and for its insistence on dissolving all paradox into 'organic unity' (where Deconstruction keeps the paradox and calls it aporia), its discipline of close reading should not have been thrown away with the politico-philosophical bathwater. It's true the New Criticism concentrated on poetry, and had little to say on narrative. Parallel with early Structuralism came the Chicago School (Wayne Booth as chief survivor, with his pre-Structuralist and much less dogmatic attempts at narratology), and Northrop Frye's myth analysis, not to mention psychoanalytical and sociological schools. However, the international 'university gap', as I call it, continued, few wanting to know what was going on or had gone on elsewhere: Barthes, for instance, 'invented' *polysémie* but had never heard of Empson's *Seven Types of Ambiguity* (1930) or *The Structure of Complex Words* (1951). Of course Empson's 'seven' types were somewhat illogical, overlapping, unsystematic, and would never have satisfied a Structuralist's capacity for abstract category, but oh, that close reading of ambiguity! Similarly with the Anglo-American rejection or later (with some exceptions) blind adoption or superficial use of Structuralism and/or Deconstruction, too many critics today, notably Feminists, have now fallen back on early twentieth-century or late nineteenth-century character analysis or plot summary, called content-analysis to show that Formalism is being rejected. And even when it is not, when, say, 'Literary Theory' or 'the Signifier' are loudly assumed and pleaded for, in practice the criticism remains with the signified. As if nothing had happened from the pre-Twenties on except perhaps the Freudian and Marxist schools, with a bit of Nietzsche or Benjamin or what have you thrown in. But why move wholly back? Why not keep the best from all systems, plus native genius if any?

As Frank did. All that excitement now seems very distant. But what was already strong in his criticism was further strengthened by the discipline of these other ways of thinking, yet never muddled or superficial. What he thought too alien to his own thought he didn't touch, he didn't force his own elegance. The small contradictions I opened with remain in the character, never in the writing. The Books not the Man from Man.

His memoir tells of them quite openly: his early initiation to research, for instance, as one of the 'minions' who proofread and checked all the references of his first professor's article on Ben Jonson's *Hymenaei*. I trust things have evolved since those days and that professors don't have minions to do their tedious work. It would certainly have been inconceivable in *soixante-huitard* Vincennes (or perhaps men professors did whereas women professors couldn't or wouldn't? I certainly would never even have thought of it). But I don't believe

Frank did either. My point however is not social, but to highlight his wise and experienced insistence on just the sort of donkey-work that nevertheless enables one, in a flash, to understand some subtle point one's slave student wouldn't even have noticed. For Frank's description of this initiation is set against his appreciation of having learned just those tedious necessities. In his preface to *History and Value* (1989) he exclaims: 'Once again, it seems unreasonable to have had such a good time while engaged on the normally quite painful process of writing a book.' The pain, the good time, the slight guilt at the good time. In a recent letter, while engaged in a commissioned book on Shakespeare, he tells me:

I can't WAIT to finish this book and send it off to its fate, with all its imperfections on its head. However, really reading Shakespeare has, I grudgingly admit, been a bit of a revelation. Nobody else ever seems to talk about the verse, or more generally about the rhetoric, except in a very academic way. I find myself stunned by HAMLET (at my age, after teaching Sh. for over forty years). I'll probably go crazy when I get to LEAR. But I must get to it very soon. The option of dropping it isn't, I fear, available whether the book is any good or not ...

And, six weeks later:

... I've been sunk in this terrible book and it must be finished and sent to New York in six weeks or so. The strain of it has a bad effect on sleep ...

The paradox of (hateful) work = stunned enjoyment is common to all writers. Only Frank would continue to express it as a revelation, clearly and elegantly, as he moves towards his eightieth birthday. As one old lady in Provence, a neighbour, said to another old lady: 'Joyeux anniversaire, et beaucoup d'années après'. And I must add, for his charming pride-side: 'et beaucoup d'honneurs après.'

Christine Brooke-Rose

34. DOUBTING THOMAS

I ONCE SENT FRANK a postcard of a painting of
Doubting Thomas putting his finger into the wound
in Christ's side; I didn't mean anything particular by
it, as far as I remember, but when Frank sent me a note
in reply, he thanked me for the image, writing that he'd
always taken Thomas to be the true patron saint of
critics. I was surprised, for I never would have seen
Kermodian scepticism in a mythical or religious perspective: to me he was, ever since I first met him in 1969, a
thoroughly modern apostle of literary appraisal. It was
Frank who, when I asked him who might be interesting
to read, answered, without missing a beat, 'Jacques
Derrida. Try *La Carte postale*.' It was 1980, the book
was just out, and I'd never heard of Derrida (nowadays
Frank often sounds as if he wishes *he'd* never heard of
him).

Doubting Thomas, with his probing finger and his
sceptic's probity, does however offer a clue to the inspir-
ing, refreshing, provocative mental ambience of Kermodian questioning. When I think back over our conversations, I hear him quietly putting a slant on things
that unsettles routine responses, throws up challenges,
lights the spark of doubt that will, if properly explored,
take you farther along in questioning a book, a stanza,
an experience, from which disturbance of assumptions
new discoveries can be made. His voice, his manner, that
contented drawing on his pipe, the level, flattish Manx
intonation, the steady eyes reflecting quiet, inner ironies,
his prevalent spoken mode of tentative inquiry rather
than statement, can mislead one into missing the devastating impact and penetration of his critical mind. His
brand of doubt doesn't blast and wither its objects of sus-
picion, as some exhibitionist performers of criticism like
to do, but I can't help feeling that if he'd probed Christ's

side, he wouldn't have left it at that, but gone on to ask why it was that Christ didn't flinch, what kind of body (what kind of text) can exist that feels no pain when you touch its wounds.

Doubt for Frank is the first principle of discernment, but his use of it doesn't place him, in his own estimation, in any superior position; its experimental results leave him in a state of bemusement. For a man who is so brilliant, so authoritative in his judgements, so erudite, and so incisive, he's always given an extraordinary impression of rueful, regretful, besetting puzzlement.

When I first met him, he was one of the judges of the Booker Prize, then in its first year. Stephen Spender was also on the panel, and he'd convened the judges' meeting in his cottage in the garden of Michael Astor's country house, Bruern Abbey, near Oxford. I was staying there for the weekend (I was going out with Jamie, Michael's son), when Rebecca West, Bill Webb, Frank and Stephen Spender came up for meals fresh from their wrestling with the shortlist. They weren't sworn to secrecy, in those days, and as we sank into the silken cushions and deep sofas after a Sunday lunch cooked by Michael's French chef, and great draughts of Portuguese rosé from terracotta bottles, conversation about the books – and about their authors, whom they mostly knew personally – grew lively: Iris Murdoch had published *The Nice and the Good*, Muriel Spark *The Public Image*, and Nicholas Mosley, who'd recently had a popular success with *Accident* (a terrific Pinter screenplay for Joseph Losey), had brought out one of his elliptical, puzzle novels, *Impossible Object*. It was all rather intoxicating for me to listen to Rebecca West, with her shrewd, cutting voice and her teddy-bear button eyes behind different pairs of spectacles on elaborate jewelled chains. But what struck me most powerfully then was the intensity of attention Frank Kermode was bringing to the mostly accessible and enjoyable productions of contemporary fiction. I knew him to be a professor most high, a Shakespearian scholar and an unparalleled interpreter of difficult, American poetry. None of the tutors I'd come across in my time of studying at Oxford had shown the slightest bit of interest in the work of living writers, let alone writing that could reach a mass audience, that anyone might read in the ordinary course of things (Iris Murdoch's fiction was never discussed as literature, though the Sapphism and general polymorphous perversities of her characters caused widespread speculation). It was Frank Kermode – with a few others, like his close friend Tony Tanner – who acted as the pioneering surveyor of a new landscape of English literary studies (naturally he often now appears stricken with doubt and filled with rue about the way the plantings have taken and grown).

That year, Frank was reading the Booker novels closely; all the time I've known him, this concentration on the notes within the larger plan, this scrupulous alertness of ear has always startled me out of inattention. Recently, after I'd been to a production of *Measure for Measure*, and we were talking about Isabella's passionate eloquence, Frank quoted Claudio saying of his sister's gift: 'For in her youth / There is a prone and speechless dialect, / Such as move men.' 'Prone and speechless,' he repeated. 'It's wonderful – but what does "prone" mean?' The *Riverside* edition, which is one of the many great Kermode opera, footnotes it with lots of question marks, 'eager?', 'apt?', 'supplicating?' I've been puzzling about it since, and wanted to write to Frank and ask, could it be a Shakespearian Gallicism, from *éperon*, spur – her eloquence the sort that spurs you on?

Such niggling cruces aren't the prime matter of Kermodian doubt, of course, just part of its wide, deep scrupulousness. He takes questioning very far: I once met Frank in New York at a party on the Upper East Side, where one of the other guests was Frank Reeve, a colleague in the English department at Columbia, who was talking with gleeful irony of his peculiar new role in life as father to Christopher, then in full splendour and vigour as Clark Kent/Superman. Both Franks were playing up to the company, revelling in a charade of geriatric self-deprecation as they contemplated the younger generation's explosion into stardom. Yet Frank K. was then immersed in his great investigation into the Bible as literature – which resulted in the unrivalled *Literary Guide to the Bible* – and was teaching himself Hebrew to that purpose. 'It's no good,' he said, 'trying to read the Bible as a book if you can't read it in the original.'

I hope it won't be too indiscreet to record here, on the occasion of his eightieth birthday, a moment when I remember Frank in the very grip of a state of doubt so consuming that he seemed set askance to his very self, so much was he at a loss for the tools that would probe the problem: this was a poser that no amount of Hebrew or close textual work would solve. It was ten years ago, and we – his friends – were invited to celebrate his seventy years at the house in Hampstead of Alfred and Reni Brendel, where the Kermodes were staying.

I arrived. No Frank. Was he late? Detained somewhere? Anita was there, to whom he was then married, with a kind of hectic colour in her pale cheeks, moving about the party, rapidly. Terrible news. Frank had had a heart attack. That day. Too late for the party to be cancelled, so here we all were. And Frank? Frank was upstairs, in bed, stricken. Not in hospital? No, they'd let him go, but he had to keep quiet.

We partied, sort of. There are some celebrated stories of hosts who never appear, but this wasn't the same. We felt badly, but still we drank champagne and chattered; poor Frank, not even a spectre at his own feast, just an exile upstairs, the guest of honour quarantined for his own good. One by one, Anita came up to us and said we should go up, not disturb Frank, but say hello – say farewell? He needed to see his friends, at this late hour, quietly. I climbed the stairs in a state of confusion, sorrow, sympathy, bewilderment: what was I to say, at this solemn moment, to the poor patient in his critical state?

I went into the guest bedroom; it was darkened, hushed. I almost smelled camphor. But Frank wasn't in the bed. He was sitting on it, at the foot, fully clothed, and he was looking as if he wanted to have a drink, a smoke. He was also in a state of deep puzzlement. He'd been told he was very ill, but there was something wrong with this diagnosis. He sat there, disconsolate in his sequestration from his own birthday party, a child undergoing some cruel punishment, in a state of utter perplexity. When he put his finger to his own ribs, as it were, to test his failing heart, he had his doubts. But unlike Saint Thomas, he was the subject of inquiry, and he could not press his own judgement of the matter. And so he remained, upstairs, as the party went on without him.

Later, when I asked him about that melancholy evening, he looked bemused, and said, 'There never was any heart attack. It was all a mistake.' He'd been right to doubt it all along.

So I hope your eightieth will be a very merry affair, dear Frank, and that this time you'll be allowed downstairs.

Marina Warner

35. THIS AND THAT

THAT FRANK KERMODE should have played a considerable part in my life surprises me not at all, though I find it puzzling that, in however minor a way, I should have been present in his – whether as an occasional abuser of his generous attention, an erstwhile thorn in his flesh or, more recently, a companion of sorts in some tragicomically difficult moments. They were the best I could manage to come up with in the way of roles as I went over the ins and outs of my knowing him across the years, the best indeed to which I can imagine myself entitled (about the only thing I may claim without presumption to share with him is the feeling of non-entitlement, though it is inevitable that, however much I know he does, I can never quite believe he can feel this). Such as they are, it is these roles which come immediately to mind, carrying a certain conviction amid so many different recollections. The spots of memory in which, conjoining fact with the necessary truth of fantasy, I find and recreate myself with him can be given no special coherence, no pressing narrative, are just the bits and pieces of an incongruous relationship, a sporadic friendship which, as such, has afforded me more pleasure than he knows.

Its beginning might well have been its end. Early in 1971, Frank had given a Radio 3 talk on 'The Conference Game' which was subsequently printed in the *Listener* where I happened to come across it. What had prompted the talk was a select interdisciplinary gathering to which he had been invited in Paris and its substance was a series of reflections on conferences in general and this one in particular, inasmuch as it not only exemplified the expectations and failures of such gatherings but also provided an intellectual basis for thinking about them. The significant framework of this conference, that is, had been the developing work of Barthes and Derrida, the Post-Structuralist account, as it was coming to be called and as Frank relayed it, of meaning and interpretation: of the impossibility of grounding the former other than in – other than as – the fictions of the latter's projections of determinate meanings. Conferences demonstrate only too well, Frank explained, that the desire to conclude, to arrive at some final truth, is always disappointed; ritually, they play out the pattern of this desire and its non-fulfilment, successful only in terms of whether they turn out to be less rather than more disappointing than usual. As

I remember Frank's account, the conference he attended provided something of an additional demonstration in that the person scheduled to give it the desired meaning failed to appear, staging thereby the failure of finality that he would no doubt – the awaited intellectual hero was Derrida – anyway have urged had he come.) Frank in all this was cautiously sympathetic, courteously dubitative, positioning himself as a player on the margin of what was to be seen as just another game. I, however, zealous for theoretical rigour and political resolve, fired off a letter to the *Listener* that began by welcoming with heavy-handed disapproval the fact that someone 'of Professor Kermode's stature' had decided to acknowledge this French work, proceeded to correct his 'theoretical misunderstandings' and ended by reprimanding him for not taking things seriously (like Hume avoiding philosophical delirium by quitting his study for backgammon and merriment, Frank was now and then to be found in his talk exiting the conference for a good lunch and a couple of dry martinis, behaviour which at the time I doubtless regarded as a gross manifestation of bourgeois recidivism, only to be expected from the Establishment figure that I took Frank to be).

So that should have been that. Instead of which, on the morning the letter was published, I received a call from Frank's UCL secretary announcing that he wished me to address a seminar he was running. Perhaps he may then have spoken to me himself, perhaps not; I remember only that it was somehow made intimidatingly clear how busy he was – he had, I believe, to go off for lunch with Borges (lunch again) – and that I, barely a graduate student, was left with a feeling of considerable apprehension. Two or three months later, still apprehensive, I thus turned up at the seminar and gave a presentation which spilled over into its next meeting too. Except for his disarming kindness (if intimidation had been an effect, it had obviously not been an intention), I can recall little of Frank on those initial occasions, which is partly the result of the years gone by but also of the nature of the seminar and of his position in it. Relatively informal, with diversely interested participants, including visitors from outside the circle of his – extremely good – English department students (invited speakers were prone to continue to attend as regular participants, as indeed I did myself), the achievement of the seminar depended more than anything on Frank's skill at creating a space that was, in a word that indicates a mode of human dealing he values and himself typifies, eminently civil, open to the recognition and critical consideration of new work in a way that, with no predetermined agenda, allowed for genuine exchange, for the emergence of positions, ideas, understanding (such civility was the reality of what I had been bent on rejecting as the evasive absence of proper purpose in the tone of the radio talk).

This is often and characteristically taken by Frank in his own recollections of the seminar to mean that he had little to do with its success, that he was merely there on the sidelines, no more than a provider of space and time, but, of course, it was he who made the seminar, who committed it so effectively to debate, who posed the necessary questions and ensured its constantly productive critical edge. If the seminar was an exceptional source of intellectual excitement, this was dependent on Frank's guiding presence, however discreet his manner may have caused that presence to seem and however much that enabling discretion may make it difficult today adequately to recall the full extent of his contribution.

In connection with which, it is important to remember too that his work at the time, and prior as well as subsequent to the seminar years, was engaged with many of the issues that the theories and ideas coming out of France were raising and newly shaping; the studies in the theory of fiction that made up *The Sense of an Ending* (1967), which I read not at all coincidentally while attending Barthes's S/Z seminar, are clearly concerned with – and contain original explorations of – just those issues. That Frank mostly insists on remembering his book as having been rendered instantly obsolete by the French work, is an expression of personal character rather than a matter of fact; his interest in elaborating a general theory of fictions ran alongside the work of Barthes and Derrida (hence the context for my reading *The Sense of an Ending*), influenced by them and others but pursuing a course of its own, as the later essays collected in *Essays on Fiction* (1983) well enough show. It was this independent but receptively enquiring interest that established the nature of the seminar and provided its vital stimulus.

As Frank later saw it, the literary and interdisciplinary theory with which the seminar engaged was another country in which he went to live without ever feeling truly at home, increasingly drawn indeed to note the limitations of imagination and response as that theoretical work was hardened with academic success into a tiredly repetitive 'Theory', locked in pointless celebrations of its own validity – 'drugged with self-regard', as he once put it. Significantly, Frank as teacher and critic founds no school, has students not disciples (no Kermodians!). His occupation – his country – is the reading of literature, with reading and literature held to strongly as values. The conflation of criticism with interpretation and the insistence on the latter as the recognition and realisation of a textual plurality which no given meaning or reference of a text is there to close has been an essential part of his framework of reflection at the same time that he has refused to come to a stop in such a position, to rest content with what have become its own easy certainties. On the contrary: learning from and responding to the modern theoretical work, he has sought to continue to involve criticism in thinking about questions of the judgement of interpretations and of the evaluation of literary works as such. However theoretically difficult it may be, the point is to acknowledge in every sense of the word a distinction of literature and to hold it to a truth that is the experience of its 'human occasions' – 'The poem is the cry of its occasion', as Wallace Stevens, Frank's great reference-poet, puts it in 'An Ordinary Evening in New Haven'.

So Frank in his teaching and writing is concerned with knowing books well, making people understand what it is to value works, prompting us to literature. Everyone will have their own instances of his having done this: he gave me *The Tempest* through the sheer brilliance of his Arden edition; Stevens's poetry through his pioneering book on him; *Loving* and *Between the Acts* which we read in the seminar and which he discussed with a brilliance of insight and appreciation that has stayed with me as the model for the reading and teaching of literature; Larkin's 'Unfinished Poem' and the cry of its last line of which he talked quietly and movingly one evening with myself and Tony Tanner; these and more, too numerous to list here. It is Frank's example in this that has taught me much and that I most admire and respect in his teaching and writing; though he probably hasn't known it, and sometimes nor have I.

How absurd, then, the occasional attempts to identify him with some – often largely ignorant and imaginary – version of modern theory and indict him for supposedly giving up on values (on literature, scholarship, truth, humanity ...). The high – or rather, low – point of this was the MacCabe affair which we went through together (as we did more interestingly through its prelude: a carefully considered, hard-worked attempt to produce a coherent, educationally responsible reform of the Cambridge English undergraduate degree course and its teaching; fear of which proposed reform provided some at least of the shameful impetus for the affair). It was the only period when I have been institutionally close to

Frank, caught up with him in day-to-day struggles and interventions; a depressing time in which, despite the stupidity and malice, much of it and most virulently directed at him, Frank gave the most constant and loyal support, put himself more than anyone else on the front line. Apart from that, which was a great deal, what I now like to remember, more marginally and with a certain embarrassment, was the role I took up as his 'writer', in the subordinate naval sense, drafting letters for him on the basis of my unfortunate talent for elaborating knotty adversarial arguments using whatever regulations, standing orders and so on might be tractably to hand. Frank had more beneficial things to do and write, so for a while, confronting the perversity of the Cambridge English faculty of the day, I did letters and drew up documents for him, just as he had once for his mad naval captains (not that he showed the slightest sign of madness; on the contrary, he was sanity in the midst of folly). He bore it all – bore me – with a resigned patience that only occasionally let through the bitterness he felt at the slings and arrows of this outrageous fortune to which, I had to reflect, I was only the more stubbornly exposing him. Be that as it may, what cannot be doubted is that to have gone through that whole period was, to adopt the idiom of Frank's Navy days which I have found so ser-viceable since learning it, to have been indeed in a 'fucking northeaster' that unremittingly blew its infamous worst (the naval chapter of *Not Entitled* stays vivid in my mind as a wryly humorous masterpiece of autobiographical writing).

My admiration for Frank as a person increased during that bad time which showed me qualities in him I had not before had occasion to witness. To respect for his learning, critical intelligence and love of literature, I added a keen appreciation of his fundamental decency, to use an indicatively – and sadly – old-fashioned term: he had every reason not to become involved in the affair, but then what had gone on was simply unacceptable, indecent, could not be left by him without response. There are also, however, traits through which ties are made that underpin admiration with something more intimate, and separate too from friendship, something which is rather the fact of this individual sustaining in one's life an idea of oneself that he or she helps, for better or worse, to represent (the individual in question need have no awareness of this). Freud talks of partial, limited modes of identification which borrow 'a single trait' – *einziger Zug* – from their object, and what I borrowed from Frank, my point of identification, was, as suggested earlier, exactly his non-entitlement (as I later came to call it after *Not Entitled* appeared): the sense that one is always out of place, that nothing is deserved.

Recalling his Manx childhood, Frank remembers a Scottish shipyard worker who presented him with the Pelican volumes of Shaw's *The Intelligent Woman's Guide to Socialism, Capitalism, Sovietism and Fascism*: 'a work which, on reflection, I should have to list, in the improbable event of someone requiring me to do so, among the forces that have shaped me, insofar as I can claim shape'. It is a typical sentence, and one which in my own fashion I constantly rewrite; with its immediate qualifying clauses of wan self-retreat, its shying away from the suggestion of any import of himself (he once told me – and it is typically his story – of a visit to a Cambridge college library where he enquired whether, but he supposed not, he might look at its *Troilus and Criseyde* manuscript and, as he had determined he would be, was told he couldn't, it wasn't for public display; that he might have said who he was, mentioned he was a scholar rather than a random passer-by, let alone declared himself to be the University's King Edward VII Professor of English, never occurred to him – after all, what real entitlement did he have?).

There is too a comic aspect to my identification which

depends precisely on Frank's ignorance of it and concerns our shared hopelessness in dealing with the practical matters of the domestic world (hopelessness at any rate as each of us individually believes it in himself). This he necessarily cannot recognise in me – it is after all his trait – and his failure to do so has had the effect of forcing me intermittently to exhibit – or give the semblance of exhibiting – capabilities to which in other circumstances I could not begin to lay claim and which, even could I, would be anyway overridden by my own perfectly Kermodian certainty that any action I might perform would serve only to make things worse. Fixed in his reflection of my kindred hopelessness but faced at the same time with his projection of me as his opposite in this, I have been impelled to perform for him what are, from his – and my – point of view notable exploits (the wish not to disappoint his faith in me wins out over actual incompetence); 'exploits' that from anyone else's point of view amount to the unremarkable accomplishment of ordinary chores: mending fuses or dealing with removal men or taking down curtains (luckily, I have so far been called upon only at this rudimentary level; my true incompetence remains unexposed).

For a while one day, I stood with him in the Luard Road house in silent contemplation of a heavy curtain which he had begun to take down to have cleaned but which, judging the enterprise over-ambitious, he had abandoned midway, leaving it desolately half-hanging, pelmet askew, resistant, so it seemed, to any further human intervention, like the shrouded furniture in Dombey's shut-up mansion. But I took it down, to his slight amazement, perhaps. I remember too when I was living in California driving down from the north to visit him in the house in Pasadena provided for him during his period at Caltech. We went to a supermarket for some minimal shopping and, as he reached for a rather banal bag of coffee, I asked why he didn't buy it fresh, pointing to the array of varieties of loose beans. But he wouldn't, he said, be able to grind it. I pointed to the extremely large grinding-machine. He looked dubious. But I ground some anyway, to his bemusement, possibly ironic, possibly not.

Hesitation as to whether or not Frank is being ironic is an experience I have often and it seems to me that a certain refusal – intentional or unintentional or both at once – quite to indicate whether he is being wholly serious is characteristic, is a strategy of his mode of being. In this connection, I am often perplexed as to Frank's presentation of himself and the gap between it and what on all other evidence, and on any rational assessment, would appear to be the real state of affairs (he could surely do all those practical things just as well as I can and indeed do them better). What I am certain of, however, is the deep-rooted dubiousness as to the even minimally successful outcome of anything. Frank lives in the belief, which I too espouse, that most things will inevitably go wrong, that decisions taken will almost invariably turn out to be mistakes, and that one's – Frank's (and my) – course in life is a series of generally predictable but uniformly inescapable accidents. Not much more, if anything, can be said than that things are as they are and can be pretty much counted on to get worse. So it is natural that Octavius's lines in *Antony and Cleopatra* should be a favourite quotation of his: 'But let determined things to destiny / Hold unbewail'd their way.' In the face of the loss of a significant portion of his library, fed to the maw of a Cambridge City Council Waste Disposal Services compacter vehicle, Frank's attitude as we stood in the sunshine, surveying rescued volumes strewn over his front lawn, ripped and soiled, was one of sorrow, yes, but also of wan acceptance – something like this was bound to happen, to happen to him, and his concern was that I might be unduly upset, might not appreciate that determined inevitability of things not reasonably to be bewailed. At such times, Frank can make misfortune – his misfortune – appear so trivially normal, so flatly fitting, that understatement is the only true response, a subdued recognition of the melancholy, the farce, the banality of it all: this is just how things are (perhaps one reason why he cites Beckett's *Comment c'est* as the most difficult book he has read – Beckett, that is, comes too close).

It is instances of this kind that crystallise my affection, these and others that intensely carry the sense for me of the incongruous relation, the sporadic friendship (in the improbable event of my having a right to the term 'friendship'). Not much of this may correspond to any reality of Frank in others' eyes, or indeed in his own, as on the whole it probably won't. But it is thus, incidentally, that I know him; in the margins, which is where – and why – such instances mean for me, such images as these.

For a single person, the Pasadena house was very large. Frank seemed unsure as to how many rooms there were and gave the impression that there were many he had never entered. Other than that, I remember little about it, since we sat up drinking most of the night I stayed there and I have no recollection of having, as I suppose I must have done, tumbled into bed in one of those unknown rooms. What does remain for me is the vision of Frank on the front porch as I left: out of scale, solitary, eager to get on with his day's writing but vaguely lingering, opaque but suddenly making me realise how glad I was to know him ('The way a look or a touch reveals its unexpected magnitudes', Stevens in 'Prologues to What Is Possible').

For good reasons, the details of which are not here important, I found myself very late one night not so long ago breaking into Frank's flat. I was, I have to say, petrified. It was not so much that he might rush at me in self-defence with whatever makeshift weapon might be to hand (though this would have been entirely understandable behaviour, I thought it unlikely), but rather that I feared the shock might be too much for him (it certainly would have been for me in his place). I opened the front door, waited on the threshold and then advanced slowly down the hallway, loudly and ludicrously proclaiming that there was no need to worry, that it was only me (it of course crossed my mind that this might well be the worst news of all, far from reassuring). I knocked on the bedroom door, went in and found Frank sitting on the bed in his pyjamas, somewhat puzzled but not manifesting overmuch surprise. 'How did you get in?' he asked. I told him. 'Oh well,' he said, 'we'd better have a drink.'

'There was this and that intended to be recognized', writes Stevens, again in 'Prologues to What Is Possible'. The remarks and recollections here have been just 'this and that'. If nothing else, they have their personal necessity for me, something at least of which, hopefully, will be recognised, Frank, by you.

Stephen Heath

36. THE KERMODE BEAR

I HAD THE PLEASURE of being introduced to Frank Kermode in the spring of 1969. We were supposed to get some work done together: I was seeing to the American publication of a series of books he was editing plus, from time to time, some books he wrote himself. That was thirty years ago. Would he agree to call it a friendship, ever since? A colleagueship from time to time? My computer's spell-check would like to call him Comrade. Perhaps it was a cordial adversarial sort of thing; his view of publishers is not unlike John Locke's, so it would be presumptuous for me to make any claims. Still, for me it has been a treasured experience, an incomparably instructive and hilarious companionship; there are few people in the world I care so much about. But he doesn't know that.

Has it been more through letters – meaning epistles, of course, but also type – or more in the actual personal encounters, this friendship (I dare call it)? A scholar of Frank Kermode's precision and elegance, a teacher of his acuity, would encourage a still bumbling student like me to gather the facts before answering this question. Still, a person of Frank Kermode's tendencies will understand when I explain this is not possible: I went to my files to reread, under K, the letters we exchanged from the spring of 1969 on – perhaps I could then cite the devastating instructions, the witty asides, the gossip, and so on, for the delectation of this volume's reader(s) whoever they may be – but the file was missing. I shouldn't have been surprised. A Kermode-like sideways disappearance act. There's a file for *Not Entitled* and one for Shakespeare, but all the others have gone. Where the classic or the modern masters or anything in between? Damnation. No doubt this vacancy will relieve him.

Anyway, how could one measure those lost letters against the uncounted and uncountable memories of the slightly weird but entertaining Italian 'business' lunches with his fellow Celt Alan Williams, and the strolls before and after, along East 59th Street; of the rowdy dinners in Brooklyn Heights with contentious pals arguing with him about music ... (My memory is uncertain here: I remember Frank insisting that the Cavatina in the opus 130 quartet was the Music One Most Wants to Hear Last. Noisy dispute erupted about the merits or demerits of the Top Ten, everyone talking at once, and I remember him lighting his pipe and chuckling at implausible views, and asking mildly, without anyone hearing him, 'What's the matter with Brahms's Fourth?' And this leaves out Susanna in Act IV of *Figaro*.) Of lectures here there and everywhere, with minor academic barons whiffling up to the dukes who insist on taking charge of our

Prince of Criticism, which is entertaining music-hall stuff, amusing to watch – and then the perfect perform-ance at the lectern, like a flawless emerald set in paste. Ineffable, sticky bits of work to get through with pecu-liar pseuds and intrusive wannabes, where his common sense and shared amusement at the inevitable ludicrous confusions did wonders. The strange, reposeful yet somehow hectic New England summer interludes. The telephone calls from Houston or other impossible cities, reporting on local oddities and customs, as if from the Trobriand Islands. The rebukes, gentle but firm, for mis-takes and errors in the publication of texts he cared about. The endurance of trials on the commercial-inter-view mass-media circuits: 'I have tried to be charming.' His cool response to a reviewer of his memoir who 'couldn't match the self-portrait with the author he'd known, but then he was never meant to.' And (this from a miraculously unlost letter) 'In fact, it seems to me I could write another memoir without repeating anything in this one. A different, possibly more sinister, personali-ty might emerge.' (I like the 'might'.) A springtime walk in the Fellows Garden at Trinity, which he has reason to remember better than I, since I was merely Playing a Role and Speaking a Part, whereas he was truly at work – and the sacred confidences between writer and editor go with me to the grave.

So the memories are plentiful: the many moments – I can't place the places, always – when the head goes back and the wonderful laugh lights up the room, or the pre-cisely modulated comment pulls a chaotic conversation into focus, or the shapely anecdote comes to rest right in the middle of difficult conversational terrain – like a lunar landing module, advanced technology deployed with eerie effectiveness, fierce but quiet. The strong polit-ical views are but rarely expressed, though I am pleased we discovered a shared enthusiasm for the feisty early Tony Benn. A republican at heart, of course, and dependably anti-English in ways I've been brought up to respect. Very beautiful vowels. Expressive eyebrows. Nice pipe. Terrifying reticence. One can never measure up to this.

Still, the letters (in both senses) matter, words on the page counting for so much. No epistolary small talk, however: to a banal inquiry some years ago as to the Christmas holidays, the reply was, 'Christmas is over, the way I like it to be.' Spring is evidently no more favoured: 'Daffodils, the bard reminds us, come before the swallow dares and take the winds of March with beauty. They can have the winds of March, for my part.' Summers make for more disappearance acts: to Italy, it would seem, or to other non-English points unspecified. (Even on holidays the steady accomplishment of brilliant literary work continues: amazed mutters about this have bubbled around New York and surrounds for decades, ever since the Trillings told everyone how daunted and perplexed they were by the terrifying number of critical essays Frank managed to complete during his Sicilian vacation with them, and yet also be in full celebratory holiday mode.)

Frank wrote to me recently in the characteristic tone. 'Pester on,' he said. I took this as a good sign, though hardly subtle, which his letters usually can't help being; a nice encouragement to keep on worrying about words on the page. I'm supposed to do this on behalf of general readers. Very funny. Otherwise known as 'general readers, in their inconceivable stupidity', as Frank noted Conrad called them ninety-three years ago; since then, they're supposed to be quite dead. I believe he finds me suited to the task of representing this group. But anyone can see the fine form of attention that Frank has always paid to the complex dynamic by which public enthusiasms, capabilities and ambitions evolve in relation to what writers are writing. And he is up to his elbows in the work of ensuring that this be done as intelligently and intelligibly as possible. If the reader is deaf, blind or moribund, then the reader must be cured, healed, resuscitated, if not resurrected. Like a good doctor, Frank first does no harm, which is more than you can say for most critics, and of course he restores his readers to vigorous good health. So despite his scepticism he is devoted to publishing – 'and please make it clear,' he insisted to me, that the enterprise is 'not for horrid profs'.

I have little to say – a Kermode locution I have vainly tried to banish from his books – about the rare white subspecies of black bear known as the Kermode bear, in which I failed to engage Frank's interest. Yet it is worth noting – another phrase that gets a check mark in the margin – that the Kermode bear comes from an island, as Frank does, does not resemble the other bears on that island or adjacent islands, and is marked by salient features that put it in vivid opposition to other members of its extended family: surely this is a Kermode. (I understand that the Kermode bear is so friendly and kind, unlike its territory-defending bad-tempered black-bear cousins, that it even allows one to tickle it between the toes, but this is not to the point.) To bombastic, easy self-praise Frank counterposes modest, ferocious hard work; to local and provincial restrictions an insistence on the limitless possibilities of literature; to competitive posturing an unforced kindness; to banal goodwill an implacable insistence on telling the truth (though what does that mean?); to the grizzly growls that sound from all too many works created by the critical tribe, a prose style of polar-white clarity and visibility.

Enough. Not the right fiddle-bow for this instrument. Enough, rather, to celebrate the rare and improving lives of this marvellous man, and to raise a glass in festivities that, I hope, endure – as his work and self will – well into the millennium to come.

Elisabeth Sifton

Unlike Frank, William Allingham never finished his autobiography. But, just like the 'Man to Man' section of *Not Entitled* – surely the best revery over childhood and youth since Yeats's – his fragment registers where the weather is. Allingham begins with extraordinary sureness of tone in his native Ballyshannon.

The little old Town where I was born has a Voice of its own, low, solemn, persistent, humming through the air day and night, summer and winter. Whenever I think of that Town I seem to hear the Voice. The River which makes it, rolls over rocky ledge into the tide; before, spreads a great Ocean in sunshine or storm; behind stretches a many-islanded Lake.

His experiment never got beyond thirty pages or so, but it was enough to fire Yeats's *Reveries* which remember 'little of childhood but its pain'. For Yeats found in Allingham 'the entire emotion for the place one grew up in which I felt as a child'. On Allingham's death he remarked

Time will take but little toll from his best lyrics; they are a possession for Ireland for ever. His native Ballyshannon will some day be very fond indeed of this child of hers, and may even be a place of literary pilgrimage some day. He will make the little town he loved very familiar to the twentieth century, the little town he sang of so wistfully:

> A wild west Coast, a little Town,
> Where little Folk go up and down,
> Tides flow and winds blow:
> Night and Tempest and the Sea,
> Human Will and Human Fate:
> What is little, what is great?
> Howsoe'er the answer be,
> Let me sing of what I know.

In Ballyshannon, Allingham received news of his appointment as Controller of Customs at Ramsey, Isle of Man, and his diary records 'Last Sunday here – for how long?' On 3 July 1849 he arrived in Douglas, where the 'gentlemanly and clever' collector, Baldwin, warned 'it's a queer place – a very queer place!' On his second day Allingham observed the Court of Tynwald. 'Wearisome' public drunkenness followed the ceremony, but Manx horses could 'manage their drivers' and delivered him back to Ramsey. After twenty days he escaped on leave to London, itself no paradise – 'Cholera bad', Carlyle and Leigh Hunt away, and only Coventry Patmore at the British Museum Library helpful and hospitable.

Back in Ramsey on 4 September, Allingham found an 'unexpected letter' appointing him to the Sub-controllership of Customs in Ballyshannon, and by 15 October, in some dodgy weather, he and his Manx kitten finally got away, after his first and last whisky toddy on the 'Bibulous Island'. He had hitherto 'never drunk a drop of alcohol in Mona, partly from economy, but more to keep at arm's length the continual incitement to liquid excess'. Drink is the background subject of his longest diary entry:

Ramsey, October 10 [1849]Walk on shore – into coffee room: characteristic island scene: Mr G. at table, a plate of sandwiches before him, nodding stiffly off his chair with half-closed eyes: T. asleep on the sofa. I waken G. for half a minute, when he goes to sofa and lies down, half on T., half on a chair. I sketch them. Landlord comes in. 'When you've done with them I want to get 'em off.' Sketch done, I waken them with a tune on the poker and fire shovel: G. puts a bed-chamber candlestick twice on his head before he is convinced it is not his hat; they get away somehow. Island of Trinculos and Calibans, no Prospero, alas no Miranda.

'Just like Ireland' had been Allingham's first impression of Man. How could he have been so wrong? Its voice, to a non-native Celt, proved hostile when not inaudible. He moved on, after Ballyshannon, to the 'morose duty' of the customs in Coleraine, gave that up to try the literary life in London, but that too failed by 1854. Returning to the customs in Ballyshannon, he could never make up his mind, and stuck it out in various English ports.

Not Entitled registers a profound sense of distance and difference, and Frank's other essays on Man also address the condition that Allingham had never really managed to choose – exile.

You left the island if a war made it necessary, or – rarest of exigencies – to go to college or university, and were expected in any case to come back as soon as you could. Indeed it was close to unthinkable that you might think of not coming back. Yet the mesh of family life and social relationships was so fine that any tear, whether caused by death or disgrace, including the disgrace of emigration, was soon mended. The idea of living anywhere else can never have occurred to my parents. I'm not sure when I first entertained it, though after my own war was over I had long been quite sure that I had to choose exile. It was, to a Manx of the time, a perverse and inexplicable choice. For a while when I was over on a visit people would stop me in the street, a man of thirty or so, and express surprise that I should still be a student. What other reason could there be now for my long absences? Then as time passed and my visits grew less frequent, the mesh was mended and nobody knew me at all.

Yeats and Allingham would have recognised Frank as one of those double agents who bear such knowledge in the world of 'away' or 'across'. They would have known intimately what he means by the remark that 'nothing can restore a fully Manx eye for Manx places'. The native cannot return, except with a fractured access to what can no longer be known. When Yeats went back to introduce his young wife and Sligo to each other, he could not even find the lake isle of Innisfree, by then not merely a literary landmark but a tourist attraction of his own creation. When a 'labouring man' cried out:

> you have come again,
> And surely after twenty years it was time to come

Yeats was haunted by the memory of

> a child's vow sworn in vain
> Never to leave that valley his fathers called their home.

His early novel *John Sherman* displays that sense of alienation which Frank found present in every perception of the local remembered and reconfronted, but he did not seek to 'stand in judgment' on all this until his final visitation to Sligo in 1929. He could never have put the matter with Frank's apparent imperturbability: to 'return to such a place, with only a memory of one's own native difference, is to invite unease, a mild dismay perhaps, such as must accompany a clear view, voluntarily undergone, of the road not taken'.

For Yeats's 'one clear view', he went back to the 'cleft that's christened Alt'. He had not visited that remarkable geological fault-line on the side of Knocknarea since 1895, when he had disputed the moral consequences of Wilde's arrest over the port at dinner with its owner, Cochrane of the Glen. This time it was a moment of self-arraignment. The Glen, which looks like a line of brush-wood, is a cleft in the mountain, about three-quarters of a mile long. The sides are perpendicular rock, about forty feet apart, with horizontal strata of limestone laid on each other like courses of brick-work, rising about sixty feet on one side, and forty on the other. Here, he shouted his own secret to the stone. The echo that came back was implacable: 'Lie down and die'.

> That were to shirk
> The spiritual intellect's great work,
> And shirk it in vain. There is no release
> In a bodkin or disease,
> Nor can there be work so great
> As that which cleans man's dirty slate.
> . . .

> O Rocky Voice,
> Shall we in that great night rejoice?
> What do we know but that we face
> One another in this place?

Frank tells us that Manx crabs pull each other down, but demonstrates that those who get away can't go home again without some such self-confrontation – man to man. Did the 'Island of Trinculos and Calibans' somehow send him in search of *his* Prospero and *his* Miranda?

Warwick Gould

6

SHAPING SPIRIT

The lake at Coole

38. THERE *are* KERMODIANS

THE NAME OF Frank Kermode first impinged on my consciousness in 1954, when I was an undergraduate reading English at University College, London. In our Shakespeare course we had lectures from Winifred Nowottny, who much later would be a colleague of Frank's when he occupied the Northcliffe chair at UCL. In later life, sadly, Winifred became increasingly eccentric and obsessive, and her end was tragic; but in the early Fifties she was a brilliant and charismatic teacher and we hung on her every word. She gave the impression that she was sharing with you her own latest thoughts and discoveries about the subject in hand. She read Frank's new Arden edition of *The Tempest* when it first came out and was greatly excited by its introduction, the gist of which she communicated to us in a lecture. This, we inferred, was the cutting edge of modern literary scholarship – and we were not mistaken.

In 1960 I was appointed Assistant Lecturer in the English Department of Birmingham University, and in the Easter vacation of 1961 I attended what used to be called the University Teachers of English Conference, at Cambridge. Among the principal speakers, along with W. K. Wimsatt and (I think) John Holloway, was Frank Kermode, then professor at Manchester. At this same conference I met Bernard Bergonzi, whom Frank had appointed to an assistant lectureship at Manchester. Bernard had recently read my first novel, *The Picturegoers*, and recognised the topography of the story as that of his own corner of south-east London – we had in fact grown up within a mile of each other, belonging to neighbouring Catholic parishes. Not surprisingly we became and have remained good friends. It was probably though Bernard that I was introduced to Frank at that conference, and was privileged to sit in someone's bedroom drinking whisky with him and his companions late one night. I was, as most people are, charmed by his affable manners and quick wit, but I regret to say that the only specific topic of his conversation I recall concerned the performance of his new Mini on the drive down from Manchester. The Mini was then, however, a novel and trendy vehicle, and seemed an appropriate possession for a cutting-edge scholar.

My personal acquaintance with Frank since then has been maintained principally through meetings at conferences and similar academic occasions, but he has also been an intellectual companion over the years, through his books, articles and reviews. I still remember the grateful wonder with which I read *The Sense of an Ending* (1967), a book of modest length but breathtaking scope. It was a seminal book for me, as for many others, which had the effect of extending my critical interest in the novel from a New Critical preoccupation with verbal style to an engagement with broader questions of narrative structure.

Peripeteia, which has been called the equivalent, in narrative, of irony in rhetoric, is present in every story of the least structural sophistication. Now perepiteia depends on our confidence of the end; it is a disconfirmation followed by a consonance; the interest of having our expectations falsified is obviously related to our wish to reach the discovery or recognition by an unexpected and instructive route ... So that in assimilating the peripeteia we are enacting that readjustment of expectation in regard to an end which is so notable a feature of naive apocalyptic. And ... we are ... reenacting the familiar dialogue between credulity and scepticism. The more daring the peripeteia, the more we may feel that the work respects our sense of reality.

The point may seem obvious enough today, but in 1967 it seemed like a revelation, the relaxed lucidity of the exposition making it all the more persuasive. *The Sense of an Ending* was full of such illuminations. It made me receptive to the new structuralist narratology which was to come out of Europe, and especially France, in the next decade, and which Frank himself did much to interpret and disseminate, though in a more reader-friendly style than that of the Parisian savants.

The concept of 'apocalypse' which runs like a thread through *The Sense of an Ending* proved a useful key to the understanding of much modern literature, notably D. H. Lawrence (whom Frank radically and convincingly reinterpreted), and also of postmodernism. His essay 'Objects, Jokes and Art' which first appeared in *Encounter* in its heyday (1966) is a brilliant, witty and elegant analysis of aleatory art, music and literature, which I was able to include as the last item in my reader, *20th Century Literary Criticism* (1972). It was pleasing to end this anthology of nearly 700 pages with the sentence: 'Or if it is not we really shall destroy ourselves at some farcical apocalypse.' (The antecedent sentence is: 'In the end what Simone Weil called "decreation" (easy to confuse with destruction) is the true Modernist process in respect of form and the past.')

His interest in the idea of apocalypse later led Frank into the area of biblical criticism and textual scholarship, and again I found myself learning from him – this time about texts that were almost boringly familiar from my Catholic background. *The Genesis of Secrecy* (1979) defamiliarised the gospels. As it has never been reprinted, perhaps I might quote from my review of that book in the *New Statesman*:

He himself writes as a declared 'secular' critic, yet in the end he seems more dejected than are most Christians by the discovery that the truth about the historical Jesus is irrecoverable, not (to borrow a metaphor from Conrad) inside the gospels like a kernel, but 'outside, enveloping the tale which brought it out only as a glow brings out a haze.' Kermode accepts the infinite plurality of interpretation whatever kind of text is in question, but for him this acceptance is tragic, since we interpret over and over again in quest of a truth that we know is unobtainable.

'World and book, it may be, are hopelessly plural, endlessly disappointing,' he elegiacally concludes. *The Genesis of Secrecy*, however, does not disappoint. It is exactly what one expects from Professor Kermode: elegant, incisive, expert and original. What could not have been predicted is that it would make the New Testament as interesting to the literary critic as Joyce or Kafka.

In an interview once Frank said, rather sadly, apropos of Harold Bloom, that 'there aren't any Kermodians in the world', meaning that he himself hadn't attracted disciples like Bloom (or, one might add, Leavis, Raymond Williams, Frye and Derrida). This is true in the sense that Frank has never formulated a critical 'method' or ideological apparatus which could be simply appropriated and applied by others. But many of us are covert Kermodians inasmuch as we regard him as the most accomplished literary critic of his generation, and strive to emulate his qualities in our own work.

There are three things I especially admire in his criticism. Firstly, he writes beautifully – a graceful, precise, apparently effortless prose which is always a pleasure to read. If it is occasionally difficult, that is because of the condensation of many complex ideas in a small space, not because of any academic pomposity or deliberate mystification. Secondly (and this is one reason why there are no card-carrying Kermodians), he is enormously wide-ranging and indefatigably curious in his intellectual interests. Renaissance literature, Romanticism, Symbolism, Modernism, narratology, hermeneutics and biblical criticism ... few modern academics have ranged so widely and to such effect. Thirdly, he never tries to say the last word about any of the many topics he touches upon. He is suggestive rather than exhaustive. He passes you the ball and leaves you some space to run with it, and perhaps even score, yourself. That is perhaps the most cherishable attribute a critic can have.

David Lodge

39. TO FRANK KERMODE

Dear Frank, I like reading you more than any other
    critic alive.
This must be because you're not really a critic but
    something else
The way Venice is not precisely a 'city' nor a panda
    Chinese
Nor a chimpanzee a monkey – that's not you! Your
    category is other than all these!
Stendhalian perception and Byronic poetry run through
    your so-called critical essays the way the River
    Plate runs through Argentina,
The way gold runs through that young woman's hair,
    yes, that one over there that you are noticing
(Another likeable thing about you) with the blown-
    agley dress
And the smiling perspiration, she has just finished a
    tennis match
And may be ready to play squash with you, you are
    holding a racquet
With your abidingly gifted hand that has such a
    direct contact
With your brain that it might be able to write even on
    the squash court –
But I have strayed from my subject: that strand of
    gorgeousness, of humour, of the sense of a true
    life, even of civility, in your writing
Which is found no place else. Even in your slightest
    works it is present, as in the review
Of a book about Princess Diana in the *New York Times*
From the beginning, where you say that the book is as
    thorough
'As any sane person could wish' – I was smiling
    through the rest of what you said –
To the second-to-last paragraph, and there,

Talking about the flowers brought and piled up
   for Diana
After her death, you, while I was expecting irony
And not much wanting it, surprised me another way by,
   simply, 'speaking from the heart,' as they say,
Saying 'It was impossible not to be moved.' Thank
   you, Frank Kermode. You give us an example of a
   man
Who is a complete one, who, brilliant and warm and
   funny, can peer into space as into time. Have a
   happy birthday!
Your mere presence in a room, dear friend, is something
   to celebrate –
To know that such a person is there! It makes our years.

Kenneth Koch

40. GROWING UP

I THINK I WAS first introduced to Frank on the steps
of the Senior Combination Room at King's, the week
I arrived to take up a fellowship in 1975. His reputation among left-wing Cambridge would-be intellectuals
was awesome. I mumbled something about how extraordinarily influential on my own work in Renaissance
studies Frank's *Renaissance Essays* had been (they had).
Actually, I don't really remember quite how the conversation went, but I do remember his characteristically self-
ironising response. He was not a Renaissance scholar, he
insisted with a shrug. Faced with an intellectual question
concerning the Renaissance (or anything else), he said, he
was just good at knowing who to ask.

I remember the incident clearly, because that is an
adage I've often found myself applying since, and whenever I do, I think of Frank. That's always been the way
with him, in my experience. A shrug, a disavowal, and
then an incisive, insightful remark you didn't forget. A

piece of golden advice that really works.

I took his advice. I sought out those I admired in the field and put to them the questions to which I needed answers. Above all, I listened to answers Frank himself gave to questions one did not yet have the understanding even to ask. Following a lecture on Edmund Spenser's *Faerie Queene* which we had both attended, he turned to me and remarked that someone really ought to look into what Spenser meant in Canto VI of Book I by the 'salvage nation', which worships Una as a goddess, and temporarily deflects her from her support for Redcrosse and the English Elizabethan cause. I went away and started to do so. My then graduate student, Willy Maley (now Professor at the University of Glasgow), went further and produced a PhD dissertation which permanently changed the direction of Spenser studies. Not only did Frank know who to ask, he knew how to frame the vital questions. He was adept at sending younger colleagues off on important quests for knowledge, in spite of the persona of resigned pessimism which he seemed to have adopted for convenience (perhaps to avoid being bothered by those he found tiresome) by the late Seventies.

Of course, I didn't know him during his happier intellectual days in London, although I had occasionally attended his graduate seminar at University College – it framed our intellectual agenda during my graduate years, giving us access to unfamiliar continental theorists and big arguments not to be found elsewhere in English academic life. By the time I got to know him personally, his disappointment with Cambridge was palpable, his conviction he had made a wrong move in taking the Regius Chair public knowledge. I was one of those involved in the unofficial working party he chaired, trying to devise an alternative English Tripos to replace the moribund and atrophied syllabus with which we and our students struggled. He fired us with what turned out to be a misplaced optimism that change could be effected in the midst of complacency; he steered a brilliant programme into existence. Then, he adopted his customary stance of resigned incredulity when the English faculty threw out his painstakingly honed alternative without discussion. When I was appointed to a university lectureship in 1976 he reacted to my excitement with predictable candour: 'Fine: if you really want to work in a snake-pit' – or words to that effect. Frank, as his friends know well, is nothing if not true to his given name!

It may come as a surprise to Frank, therefore, to learn that those dark days in the late Seventies when he presided like some gloomy deity over the absurd antics of the Cambridge English faculty were critical for the intellectual development of those of us (and there were many) who admired him. He taught us by example to aim high, but never to expect too much. He showed us how to be dignified in defeat. He never (so far as we knew) lost his sense of humour, his ability to rise above and wryly ridicule those ranged against him. Contrary to his own memoir of the period, I doubt there was anyone in Cambridge or in the country at large who was really in any doubt that Frank's was the finer cause, in the absurd battle to oust the forces of literary theory (alias progress) from Cambridge English around 1980. Nor that the so-called victory of the forces of ignorance and laziness was a pyrrhic one. Or perhaps the point is that what felt to Frank like defeat was an important part of his troops' process of growing up, a coming to terms with their own limitations which is (surely) a crucial part of coming to maturity. I think the most important lesson Frank taught me, though, has to do with intellectual humility. I am not, God knows, a humble person (any more, I believe, than he is). When challenged in public my instinct is to stand my ground whatever the consequences. But where research and its accompanying arguments are concerned, I have, I hope, learned always to be prepared to admit that it might be otherwise, that one might have been mistaken. Indeed, that now seems to me to be a quality in a research temperament which ensures continuing productive engagement with one's subject.

As usual, a Kermode anecdote helps make clear what I mean. Some time in the Eighties Frank and I were sitting together at a public function, whether in Cambridge or London I no longer recall. Frank had just got back from one of his trips to the United States. 'I've just spent some time with a young man who is writing a doctoral dissertation on me,' he told me, with a slightly sheepish smile (as though such an idea was faintly absurd). It was fascinating, he continued, to hear someone who had studied one's most precious ideas at length and in depth give an account of what it was one had been trying to say. There was a pause. Having done so, Frank went on, the young man proceeded to explain that in spite of the diversity of Frank's interests and output, the argument of the thesis was going to be that there had been only one brilliant idea, developed in *The Sense of an Ending* in 1967. Thereafter, Frank's intellectual biographer had explained to him that he had simply reworked that one great idea over and over again. Another pause. 'And you know what?' said Frank, with just a glimmer of a smile, 'When I went away and thought about it, he was right!' It would be nice to believe that, having achieved the eminence Frank has in one's career, one had the greatness and generosity of intellectual spirit to recount such a story of oneself.

Lisa Jardine

41. ATTENZIONE

WE MET IN Trieste. I was coming to this most northern and un-Italian of Italian cities from the south, from Rome. Frank was coming from the north – London, via Milan. We were going to hold a joint seminar in the English department of the local university, invited by a distinguished colleague of mine, Paola Bottalla. I was happy and excited at the idea of encountering Frank not as the beloved friend (Tony's and mine – I had met him through Tony Tanner; in fact, years before he had been witness at our rather sudden and tempestuous wedding), but as Professor Kermode; and sharing with him (albeit briefly, submissively) the academic stage. Coming up, on the very long train journey, I had been reading his freshly translated *Forme d'attenzione* (*Forms of Attention*, published in English five years earlier). Once again, in Daniela Fink's very good translation, Frank's voice had fascinated me with its enchanting suave and persuasive accent.

I found the little book absolutely perfect; the title inspired and brilliant, as many of Frank's titles. And, moreover, absolutely true. 'Attentive' – that's how Frank had always struck me; at the same time courteous and caring. Frank's criticism itself, it seemed to me, could truly be synthesised in the very idea of 'attention', of 'care'. It was, in fact, a way of his caring for forms, and for people. Frank was formal; his formality was part of his warm elegance: he paid attention to you, he gave you his attention, and it was never cold, as form sometimes can be. It was warm and affectionate. Human and humane.

'*Attenzione*' is a noun very much used in Italian. If you live in Rome, especially, you need a lot of it. ' *Attenzione*' – don't cross the street, not even at the zebra crossing, without having looked carefully in both directions; '*attenzione*' – don't walk with your bag like that ... Beware, beware, *attenzione*, Frank, be careful, watch out, I had kept telling him, when he stayed with me for a few days in Rome, but it was useless; of that kind of degraded, mundane attention you need in an Italian environment, Frank was simply not capable. He would walk absent-mindedly, not even noticing the dangers he miraculously escaped under my guidance.

He was, though, capable of a finer kind of attention which had nothing to do with that rather military, police-like concept of *attenzione* as surveillance and vigilance, which is the most common sense of the word in Italian.

Of course, the other sense is there, in the Latin root of *attendere*. Which takes you to 'tender' and 'tenderness' – yes, that too I had always felt: Frank's tenderness for me, his willingness to help and tend and attend and care. Years before I had brought him my one hundredth version of Wallace Stevens's *Notes Towards a Supreme Fiction*, my desperate attempt (a self-inflicted despair, since I had wanted to translate the as yet untranslated poem I loved so much) and showed him my doubts – hundreds and hundreds of impossible shades and nuances of Stevens's American-English, whose impossibility of transposition into Italian was driving me mad. We sat there in his Cambridge home and he would listen – attentive, responsive, receptive. His eyes were intent, the expression tense and tentative, as if all his being were in suspension, in attendance, or rather, in expectation that the meaning of the American poem be reborn in Italian. When he felt it had happened, he would exclaim 'that's excellent' and he would rejoice; when it did not happen, he would say 'no, not quite, don't you have a word for ...?'

No, I would explain, we who are born Italians do not have all the words Americans, or the English have; and that's why the job of the translator is so interesting and so frustrating. Especially if you don't do it as a job, but as a challenge you accept from a poet you adore. Frank understood the challenge and the despair and the fun, and was absolutely taken by the game of finding equivalents between foreign words and foreign concepts. Clearly he came to Italian via Latin, which is the best way, because it makes you aware of the infinite resonances of Italian language, that have no echo to less cultivated ears. And because via Latin, Frank came to

Italian through its roots, and roots and etyma are a very good, Heideggerian way of approaching Stevens.

But now, there we were, in Trieste, at the station, ready to go to the lecture hall. It was a grey, wet day. I was sorry. I would have wanted a sunny day for Frank, but Trieste is not my domain – I had no power so far north. It had been good, the weather, when Frank was in Rome, and in my native region, Tuscany, and now I was sorry about the rain. 'Never mind, my dear' – Frank was of course disappointed, but he would not say so. So off we went to the lecture hall, and our Shakespearian afternoon began.

I don't remember exactly what was said, but I remember the atmosphere, which was Frank's creation, because it was modulated by his voice – low-key, subtle, gentle, leading you without boasting, no showing off, no nonsense, to crucial points and through obscure lines, never leaving you there alone, always offering you the support of his immense, but immensely discreet learning.

I felt so well, so at ease. It was a real conversation, *un colloquio*; we were talking together, or rather one after the other, in a smooth flow and interchange of words and ideas, that after a short time spun a web that held us all together in a kind of thrall. Hamlet, Rosenkrantz and Claudius were there, conjured up by Frank's spell.

How could I thank Frank for this memorable afternoon? Being myself a stranger in this strange city – so literary, so full of magic – I could not give him Trieste the way I had given him Rome or the Maremma marshes, years before. Thus I mused … until over the aperitif at a café on the main square, Piazza della Borsa, chance offered me the way.

I glanced disinterestedly at the paper: was there anything on at the theatre, at the Opera House? I knew of Frank's love of music. Yes, there it was: at the solemn, neo-classical Teatro Verdi there was *Don Giovanni*. The stage director was a very dear friend of mine, Franco

Giraldi. The stage design was by Josef Svoboda. And even though the Don Giovanni was being sung by an unpronouncable Norwegian tenor, I knew and greatly admired Furlanetto, who was Leporello. I called the theatre to book. No way – the theatre was absolutely full. It was the last performance, booked out months ago. Was Franco Giraldi around? No, Mr Giraldi was away, they did not know where.

I did. I tried Franco's country home, where I knew he would be when he was not working. And there he was. And he would make sure that Frank and I had seats for the last performance.

And so we went, and we sat in the royal box and it was about right for Sir Frank Kermode. Frank adored it. Just as he adored the late after-theatre dinner at the 'Elefante bianco', and I loved it all. And thought I had had the perfect day: Shakespeare and Mozart and all sorts of attentions from and with my beloved friend.

Nadia Fusini

42. A SENSE OF TIME

A HUGE BROWN LECTURE theatre, tiered, rows of students, heads still, intent with listening. Far off, far below, small, a man speaking, quietly, gently, as he might speak to a group of friends gathered for an evening. And the hall invisibly yet palpably changing tone, colour, coming alive as he drew us along the many paths of his thoughts, gathering what was scattered in us towards a sense that was woven in a myriad of strands and textures. The empty vault of the hall becoming smaller, intimate, his voice moving us through tides and eddies of thoughts, facts, questions, always room for another question, wondering, sharing with us a breadth and depth of wandering and scholarship, a treasuring of all that might draw one further towards other voices, other rooms – a memory that seemed to hold whatever had moved it over the years, an extraordinary harvest of learning, yet always staying close to us in the questions through which he drew us along with him, making sense of the patterns and codes of our seeing, of living more deeply towards whatever we might find.

And a quiet rising within us all as we listen, travelling with him, and what seemed far off came close, within reach of our own raw and unformed worlds. Shakespeare, Marvell, Herbert, Lawrence, Donne, wherever he took us became in some way familiar, approachable, slowly, that past coming alive into the present moment, touching our own lives, the struggle and search for meaning, bringing it closer, closer. 'Fictions', he wrote in *The Sense of An Ending*, 'are for finding things out.'

I don't know what impulse made me knock on The Professor's door one afternoon. Growing up, one is never quite sure where one is going, yet something in the way he had spoken in the lecture had made the world spread out and grow. I had left school early, bored and donkeyfied in the pushing over so many too small too tight stiles of convent education. A year on a keyboard as a secretary had provoked an intense hunger to live more deeply, to go under the surfaces that seemed to shape and compel life. Knocking, entering a room with a great polished table with islands of books, books along the walls, on the chairs, in his hand. I don't remember what we talked about, but I remember his chair near the window looking out over the grey of London, the quiet warmth of his welcome, and coming away more deeply alive from whatever he moved me towards – T.S. Kuhn, Gombrich, Popper, J.Z. Young. Time with him was like taking a walk with an Indian tracker, always curious yet knowing deeply the landscape through which he moved, remarking on signs, traces, directions of wind, awakening you to all that is moving invisibly about one. And slowly – in a way I have never experienced since – the tight coils of the mind, loosening, unravelling, spreading out, as water spreads itself out over a surface, forming pools, reflecting, catching light.

To enter his room was to enter another deeper time and despite the pressures of his own work he seemed to create a sense of time, unhurried, spreading out the tangle of passion and incoherence within which I felt enmeshed. He was never impatient of questions that could not find their words, seemed always able to scent out what might shift the chaos towards a clarity – always a sense of infinite time with which to follow the drift, tracing, surfacing, treasuring. Later as a dancer I learned of the magnetic crystals within the ethmoid bones of the nose by which certain birds migrate, through which the growth of cells alter according to shifts in the earth's magnetic field, and perhaps what he taught me most in those afternoons was to sense and follow my own nose.

I remember the way his thinking, talking, could make things transparent, a seeing through to the impulse of some deeper patterning, undertows through which a life is drawn, which takes shape within the voices of literature, the living and miraculous constellations of language, images, that would make you see: illuminations, words as magic. As a child I remember climbing up high into the trees looking out on the world through the branches, thrilled by the new and secret view gained, seeing, wider, over the walls, into unfamiliar windows, comrade to the birds, looking it seemed into another world, into the same world from another point of view. Sitting and talking in his room was to experience that same sense – of what was within one's gaze coming alive, alight in the flame of his interest – and the room itself seemed to widen. He taught me that perception was not a viewing of 'out there' but a breathing in – a feeling with and into whatever one encountered. And wherever you chose to go it seemed he would go with you, notice and open yet another window, so delicately opening the patterns of one's mind. Those afternoons of quiet talking remain in my mind as among the happiest and richest memories in my life, a quality that I will never forget (the polar opposite of pedantry), of a humanity and delight in what might come, the delight of a conversation, something invisible yet essential coming a little closer to one's understanding. Somehow he had the ability to stand in the open with you, not seeming to be a teacher, though he was that in a unique way, able to guide one to live more clearly from one's own centre – a teaching that arose not from a solipsism or burrowing inwards, but from walking with you upwards, wandering, questioning, chuckling.

It is many years since I sat in those lectures, seminars, tutorials, yet the quality of them remains, the memory of his presence guiding, opening, laughing, curious, sharing a world that became spacious in the breadth of his reading and knowledge, a humanity that remains an inspiration to me. To see and feel always more deeply in to what is before you, not to be awed by the hierarchies of whatever world one encounters but to walk simply as an other human being towards whatever one encounters and to listen carefully to what is said - and also to what is as yet unformed, yet coming towards us from the darkness of ourselves. In these recent years when my own life has become so distant from that world of University College London, yet scraps of news of him reach me and I am immensely cheered knowing still of his presence who so profoundly shaped my own.

Miranda Tufnell

43 · HOPELESSLY PLURAL

THE OTHER DAY I took down from a bookshelf an old volume of Edward Young's *Night Thoughts*, written in 1742–44, which I had bought some twenty-five years ago and had never got around to reading except in bits and pieces. As I read through, coming across such lines as

O, that my song could emulate my soul

I wondered what Frank thought about Young's poetry. I didn't wonder if he had read *Night Thoughts*, and no doubt Young's plays and whatever else written by that 18th century proto-surrealist who wrote by the light of a candle stuck on a human skull, because it is axiomatic that Frank has read everything. I wondered if Frank had any high regard for Young's *Night Thoughts*, which would raise my own regard, uncertain as it was – uncertain as it always is when reading a work of literature that comes without any supportive study of it, simply because, as in the case of Young, such literature may be so neglected no study of it can be readily found. Then it occurred to me that Frank's enthusiasm for certain works of literature, modest in tone but filled with miraculously revealing insights, has so often roused my own enthusiasm. Would I have read the whole of *The Fairie Queene* without having been inspired by Frank's love for the great work, expressed not only in print, as in his Shakespeare, Spenser, Donne, but in conversation, when, in a rather light-hearted way, he would quote whole stanzas?

And Frank has not only made me aware of the great works of the past, but aware of what is going on in contemporary literature. It was Frank who, in the mid Seventies, told me about the stories of Raymond Carver, and urged me to read his first collection, *Will You Please Be Quiet, Please?*

As for giving me insights into the minds of writers, a short 'explanation' of Derrida by Frank that appeared in a newspaper and that I cut out to paste in my diary – written, Frank later told me, on the train from Cambridge to London – made me, at least while I was reading the article, understand Derrida as I hadn't been able to before, and sent me to try to read him, only to find that once again I couldn't understand. And of course I was amazed by the clarity and at the same time subtlety of Frank's understanding, which he seemingly so effortlessly, so unpretentiously and lightly communicated.

And there is the sheer range of Frank's intellectual curiosity and reading, which, as an inspiration, is a demanding inspiration. I once encountered Frank on the street near University College, he was carrying a mess of very large books on, he said, Botticelli. Excusing himself from having a drink in a pub, he was anxious to get at the books, and his excitement made me wonder what he had discovered about Botticelli. What he had discovered came out in his essay 'Botticelli Recovered', which was about Herbert Horne, one of the first men to take the painter seriously after centuries of neglect. The range of references in the essay – Ruskin, Walter Pater, Michael Levey, Ian Fletcher, John Pope-Hennessy, Arthur Symons, Ernst Gombrich, Fritz Saxl, Warburg, Michael Podro, Edward Panofsky, Hippolyte Taine – filled me with admiration and also the anguish of someone whose reading could never, ever catch up with Frank's for a true appreciation of the culture we live in.

There is a larger, deeper way in which Frank has inspired me in my appreciation of our culture – or what I believe, and what I am sure he believes, is the best of our culture, a high culture of moral and spiritual value. I say, 'I believe in a high culture of moral and spiritual value', yet, at the same time, my belief is belied by the deepening sense that that high culture I have so counted on to give meaning to my life is, like sunlit clouds I once thought to be the mysterious realm of angels, rapidly being dispersed from our sky. I find myself more and more despairing of everything I, as a writer, assumed to be of paramount interest – of paramount need – in the world of cultured people: that literature, that art, that music once gave me, if not a conviction, an enlivening sense of moral and spiritual possibility. As I lose it, I go more and more to Frank for confirmation of that sense – though, paradoxically, he might tell me that so much of his study of the high culture of literature is in fact the study of the loss.

My favourite book of Frank's is *The Genesis of Secrecy*, which I go to often. Again, he might say that I go to it for my own reasons, divining in it what I need, but then that is one of the points the book makes about readers and books. It is not a reassuring book, in that it opens one up to uncertainties much more than it defines certainties, if it defines anything that is certain. One could read it as a disperser of the angelic clouds of moral and spiritual transcendence. But when I read –

World and book, it may be, are hopelessly plural, endlessly disappointing; we stand alone before them, aware of their arbitrariness and impenetrability, knowing that they may be narratives only because of our impudent intervention, and susceptible of interpretation only by our hermetic tricks. Hot for secrets, our only conversation may be with guardians who know less and see less than we can; and our sole hope and pleasure is in the perception of a momentary radiance, before the door of disappointment is finally shut on us.

I am, however much I feel the all too justifiable meaninglessness of the world and book, also reminded that, for some reason that escapes the most positivist, the most atheistic of critics, there does always remain the need for narrative and some meaning to be interpreted from the narrative, the need to converse with the guardians of the secrets even though they may know less and see less than we can, the need for the moment of hopeful and pleasurable radiance. I look to Frank to use all that is best of our culture as evidence of a great need that has, I believe, been his great and mysterious impulse to write book after remarkable book, review after remarkable review, in which remarkable meanings are divined. Against all his self-deprecation, his feeling not entitled, his pessimism, he keeps the door of disappointment from closing, allows us to glimpse the momentary radiance. This is Frank's grandness.

David Plante

44 · A KIND OF WAR

HE WAS SITTING in his office smoking his pipe and looking, somehow, benign. I am not sure now why this was such a surprise, or even shock, to me. I had expected someone forbidding – having laboured under the firm conviction that carrying that much learning, if he was not cowed by it but bore it as effortlessly as his writing, he would at the very least look strange. So it took me a while to adjust to the fact that an almost casual lightness was to be his style and one of his gifts to me. All his best lines thrown away, almost dropped, a bit like the way he tipped the ash from his pipe and then, with the utmost concentration – as if this was where the real effort belonged – lit it again. It was the opening moment in what he had to teach me, and although I didn't know it then, the opening salvo of what, in the most productive of senses, I would discover was a kind of war.

I had been studying in Paris, stretching out a one-year French Government scholarship to two in the firm belief that, intellectually speaking – although by no means just intellectually speaking – it was the only place to be. I had returned to London to do a PhD when one of my oldest friends told me that Frank Kermode's seminars at University College were the one site in British academia where something of the spirit of what was then called 'French theory' was to be found. The one venue expansive and open-minded enough to make room for what, in so many other academic circles in Britain, was rapidly being perceived and then defined as pure threat. But since there was no way of knowing how far that expansiveness would stretch, I had submitted a proposal to University College on nineteenth-century children's fiction, based on the work of Gillian Avery, which I had hoped would make me, as someone who had been mainly hanging around in French cafés, look somehow scholarly and serious enough. And then, somewhere between my acceptance by the College and my arrival, I had begun – with a passion barely diminished to this day – reading Freud. So I walked into his office on that first day with two proposals, the one they had accepted and a new one based on Freud, Lacan and Peter Pan. As he sat there reading them over he had, I think one can fairly say without too much exaggeration, my intellectual life in his hands. They will reject the second one – it was after all not a little bit crazy – I was convinced.

That he didn't – 'The one we accepted was, frankly, rather boring', he said – allowed me to find a home back in England from which I had had far more than academic reasons to flee. I still owe him that much and always will. He fostered my love of psychoanalysis, a love that was only partly academic, and did everything he could to give me the space to follow a path which, to say the least, lacked an obvious destination. But he was of course – and still is – the master theoretician of that other, far more deadly, insanity: the belief that endings, the pat and often apocalyptic conclusion, are where any of us should ever want to be.

The war, then, was not about substance, even if our intellectual paths have so dramatically diverged over the past ten years or so, that I have occasionally sat in one of his lectures in which he rails, for love of poetry, against more recent theoretical avenues, and wondered how on earth I manage to escape unscathed. It was about language. Only when I came upon this in his memoir did I understand how much was at stake:

To love words, whatever they meant – even without knowing what they meant – more than the world, which you can't properly handle unless you have some understanding how its things work, was part of my inheritance.

And then his devotion to a kind of precision, unusually combined with such a love of words beyond meaning, his insistence – which his father called 'hairsplitting' – on forms of vital historical discrimination: the difference for example, redundant for his father since both were equally enemies for the Manx, between the English and the Jews.

When I gave him my first piece of writing, he pre-empted my response to his demand for a different type of clarity: 'You will see it as recuperation, I know.' He knew that for a certain moment of theory, refusal of common language was a must. Whether for Lacan or Barthes, the political integrity of the writing meant you had to put yourself the other side of what made, most obviously and suspiciously, sense. You had to generate the difficulty inside the writing, you had – as Lacan saw it – to speak against the ego, stop the words from tidying the unconscious away. But what I did not realise then – something which I now think Lacan himself failed to predict – is that his particular ironic gesture in language could be made only once. Twice and you have something between a formula and a nervous tic. Three times, you have founded a school. Before you know where you are, a language intended to be a critique of egos and institutions becomes one of the academy's favourite house styles. In the meetings which took place in his house in Vienna, Freud always insisted that, instead of reading a paper, everyone spoke from notes. You must win your audience.

Once you acknowledge that of course you have to start thinking about who they might be. So there was another politics to his agenda – to write in a way that might reach beyond the confines of the academy, to those outside its walls. Half jokingly, he once said to me, with a wonderfully flattening gravity, 'Always remember, or at least start by assuming, that your reader is unlikely to be as interested in what you are writing as you.'

I like to think – to pay him the compliment of difference – that I still don't write in quite the way he would choose. But if I go back to those first encounters, and the seminars which my arrival at the College gave me admission to and which he conducted with such intellectual commitment and grace, I have no doubts about how decisive they were. However much you know, what matters are the forms of communication, or forms of attention as he might say. If you carry what you know as lightly as he does, then it becomes something which other people can bear. So, often when I suggest to a student, or friend, that she or he rewrites a sentence, or when I am having the best arguments about writing, I can hear his voice. And just sometimes, I will find myself saying, 'As Frank Kermode once put it to me …'

Jacqueline Rose

English Pastoral Poetry. From the Beginnings to Marvell
(ed.), 1952
Seventeenth-Century Songs (ed., with J.P Cutts), 1956
Romantic Image, 1957
John Donne, 1957
Wallace Stevens, 1960, 1989
The Living Milton (ed.), 1960
The Banquet of Sense, 1961
Discussions of John Donne (ed.), 1962
Puzzles and Epiphanies. Essays and Reviews 1958-1961,
1962
William Shakespeare. The Final Plays (ed.), 1963
Shakespeare, *The History of Troilus and Cressida* (ed.),
1963
The Faerie Queene, I and V, 1964
Four Centuries of Shakespearian Criticism (ed.), 1965
On Shakespeare's Learning, 1965
The Sense of an Ending. Studies in the Theory of Fiction,
1965, 1967
Selections from the Minor Poems and the Faerie Queene
(ed.), 1965
Andrew Marvell. Selected Poetry (ed.), 1967
Continuities, 1968
The Poems of John Donne (ed.), 1968
Shakespeare: 'King Lear'. A Casebook (ed.), 1969
Renaissance Essays: Shakespeare, Spenser, Donne, 1971
Modern Essays, 1971
Novel and Narrative, 1972
The Oxford Anthology of English Literature (ed., with
John Hollander), 1973
Lawrence, 1973
English Renaissance Literature (with Stephen Fender and
Kenneth Palmer), 1974

Yeats and Anglo-Irish Literature. Critical Essays (ed. C.J.Rawson, with memoir by Frank Kermode), 1974

How We Read Novels, 1975

The Classic. Literary Images of Permanence and Change, 1975, 1983

Selected Prose of T.S. Eliot (ed.), 1975

The Genesis of Secrecy. On the Interpretation of Narrative, 1979

The Art of Telling. Essays on Fiction, 1983

The Bible. Story and Plot, 1984

Forms of Attention, 1985

Henry James, *The Figure in the Carpet and Other Stories* (ed.), 1986

The Literary Guide to the Bible (ed., with Robert Alter), 1987

History and Value, 1988

Shakespeare, *The Tempest* (ed.), 1988

An Appetite for Poetry. Essays in Literary Interpretation, 1989

Andrew Marvell (ed., with Keith Walker), 1990

Poetry, Narrative, History, 1990

The Uses of Error, 1990

Shakespeare, *King Lear* (ed.), 1992

Anthony Trollope, *He Knew He Was Right* (ed.), 1994

Anthony Trollope, *The Way We Live Now* (ed.), 1994

The Oxford Book of Letters (ed., with Anita Kermode), 1995

Not Entitled. A Memoir, 1996

Cleanth Brooks and the Art of Reading Poetry, 1997

Shakespeare's Language, forthcoming, 2000

CONTRIBUTORS

MIRIAM ALLOTT is editing E.M.Forster's *Alexandria* for the
Abinger Edition   AL ALVAREZ has recently published his
memoirs *Where Did It All Go Right?*   ANNE ALVAREZ is a
writer and a consultant child psychotherapist at the Tavistock
Clinic   NOEL ANNAN is former Vice Chancellor of the
University of London   BERNARD BERGONZI is Emeritus
Professor of English at the University of Warwick   LOGAN
BROWNING is lecturer in English and the Humanities at Rice
University, Houston, Texas   RICHARD BURNS's latest collec-
tion of poems is *Against Perfection*   PETER CAMPBELL
draws and writes for the *London Review of Books*   IAN
DONALDSON is Grace Professor of English and Fellow of
King's College, Cambridge   DENIS DONOGHUE's most
recent book is *The Practice of Reading*   STEPHEN FENDER
is Professor of American Literature at the University of Sussex
JOHN FORTUNE is writing a biography of George Parr with
his colleague John Bird   NADIA FUSINI's latest novel is
L'Amor Vile; she teaches at the University of Rome   WYNNE
GODLEY is Emeritus Professor of Applied Economics at
Cambridge University   ALEXANDER GOEHR is Professor of
Music at Cambridge University   WARWICK GOULD is
Director of the Institute of English Studies at the University of
London   STEPHEN HEATH teaches in Cambridge
ANTHONY HOLDEN is a Fellow of the Center for Scholars
and Writers at New York Public Library   JOHN HOLLANDER
is Sterling Professor of English at Yale University   LISA
JARDINE is Professor of Renaissance Studies at Queen Mary
and Westfield College, University of London   KENNETH
KOCH's latest collection *Straits* was published in 1998
DAVID LODGE is a novelist and playwright and Honorary
Professor of Modern English Literature at the University of
Birmingham   EDWARD MENDELSON teaches English at
Columbia University   KARL MILLER was a literary editor
and Northcliffe Professor of English at University College,
London   ANTHONY NUTTALL is Professor of English at
Oxford University   URSULA OWEN is the editor of *Index on
Censorship*   CHARLES OSBORNE was literary director of
the Arts Council of Great Britain   BRIAN PHELAN is an

Irish playwright whose plays include *The Signalman's Apprentice* and *Himself* ADAM PHILLIPS's latest book is *Darwin's Worms* DAVID PLANTE's most recent novel is *The Reign of Terror* RICHARD POIRIER is editor of *Raritan Quarterly* and chairman of the Library of America PETER PORTER's *Collected Poems* appeared in 1999 RANDOLPH QUIRK is a cross bencher member of the House of Lords with an interest in education CHRISTINE BROOKE-ROSE's latest novel is *Subscript* JACQUELINE ROSE is Professor of English at Queen Mary and Westfield College, University of London ELISABETH SIFTON is Senior Vice-President of Farrar, Straus & Giroux DANIEL STERN's latest book is *One Day's Perfect Weather: More Twice Told Tales* JOHN SUTHERLAND is Northcliffe Professor of English at University College, London EDWARD TAYLER is Lionel Trilling Professor in the Humanities, Columbia University ROBERT TEAR published his autobiography, *Tear Here*, in 1990 J.B. TRAPP was Librarian and later Director of the Warburg Institute, University of London MIRANDA TUFNELL is a dancer, choreographer and Alexander teacher JOHN UPDIKE's latest novel *Bech at Bay* was published in 1999 MARINA WARNER's most recent book is *No Go the Bogeyman* PETER WASHINGTON is General Editor of Everyman's Library and author of *Madame Blavatsky's Baboon* MARY-KAY WILMERS is the editor of the *London Review of Books*